CONSU ☜ W9-BZD-793

BUYING & SELLING

YOUR

HOME

Contributing Authors: C. Randall Pivar and Dr. William H. Pivar

This publication is designed to provide accurate and authoritative information with regard to the subject matter covered. It is written with the understanding that neither the publisher nor the authors are engaged in rendering legal or accounting advice. If legal, accounting, or other expert assistance is required, the reader should solicit the services of a competent professional in the field.

The publisher and the authors specifically disclaim any personal liability for loss or risk incurred as a consequence of the use and application, either directly or indirectly, of any advice or information presented herein.

Contents

Chapter 1:
Benefits of Home Ownership

Ask ten different people to describe their idea of the "American Dream," and you'll likely get ten different responses. At the same time, among those ten responses, chances are there will be one common element: home ownership. Owning a home has long been at the top of most Americans' list of personal and financial objectives. And, for the most part, we've been quite successful in achieving that objective: With over 60 percent of American families owning their own homes, the United States has the highest incidence of home ownership in the world. And every day, thousands more Americans join these ranks.

Home ownership is desirable because it brings very real benefits and rewards. This chapter discusses the most important ones.

FORCED SAVINGS

The cost of purchasing a home can be considered a way to save money. Here's why: Home loans are generally *amortized*. An amortized loan is paid in full over its payment period with equal payments that include both principal and interest. Each monthly payment pays the interest for the preceding month; the balance of the payment applies to the loan's principal amount. Therefore, every month the amount applied to principal increases and the amount applied to interest decreases. In the early years of a home loan, very little is applied to the principal, but in later years most of each payment serves to reduce the principal due. A home purchaser is thus forced to save, building valuable *equity*, which is defined as the difference between the market value of the home and what is owed against it.

In comparison, a renter, after a lifetime of renting, would have a stack of rental receipts as the only tangible evidence of his or her occupancy. Since rent amounts to about 25 percent of the gross income of the average renter, one-quarter of a lifetime of employment effort is expressed in that stack of rent receipts. For 40 years of employment, rent payments represent 10 years of hard work.

There is another benefit to be derived from forced savings. When a loan is paid off, the payments cease. With a mortgage loan, this is usually near or during the borrower's retirement years. This enables a retiree to have a much higher standard of living as cash is freed for discretionary spending. A renter, however, is tied to rent payments for life, with each rental increase affecting his or her living standard.

INFLATION HEDGE

One of the saddest laments is "I should have purchased that home for $ _____ ." Because of increases in value, many people regret not making a purchase when prices were much lower. Since World War II, property values have increased tremendously, the principal reason being inflation. While other investments have fluctuated widely, real estate has sustained far greater stability. While there have been plateaus in the climb in prices as well as some regional dips, real estate values have generally increased at a rate in excess of inflation. While the values of other investments have fluctuated widely, real estate has sustained far greater stability.

It is rare for a person to sell a car, jewelry, or other personal possessions for more than was paid. The benefit derived from these possessions was in the use. With real estate, you not only have the use and enjoyment of the property, but you are actually making an investment for your future. With the purchase of real estate, you guarantee yourself a price and a payment for the future, and you provide yourself an opportunity to enable your money to grow.

LEVERAGE OPPORTUNITY

Investments in stocks and bonds generally require cash. A homebuyer, on the other hand, can purchase a home with only a percentage of the total cost. While "no down payment" home purchases are possible, down payments generally range from 10 percent to 20 percent of the home's purchase price, with the balance financed by a lender for the homebuyer. This ability to use *leverage*, or someone else's money, is of great benefit to a homebuyer, especially when inflation is considered. For example, assume a homeowner buys a $100,000 home with a 10 percent down payment. The equity value at that time is $10,000. Next, assume that the market value of the home increases by 10 percent to $110,000. The buyer's equity ($110,000 value of the home – $90,000 owed = $20,000) has increased 100 percent. If the same home investment were made with cash, and no borrowing or leveraging used, the homeowner would experience only a 10 percent increase in equity or return on the initial investment. By understanding the concept of leverage, you can readily see why more investors have become millionaires from real estate than from any other type of investment.

COLLATERAL VALUE

As noted above, a homeowner's equity is the difference between the market value of the home and what is owed against it. A homeowner's equity increases as the loan principal is paid off month by month, and as inflation increases the property's value. This increased equity is a financial asset owned by the homeowner and is available to him or her to be used as needed. With increased equity, owners can refinance existing loans for their accumulated equity in cash, or they can borrow on their homes with a home equity loan or second mortgage. Borrowing on home equity, while sometimes risky, has allowed many successful business people to become self-employed. Thus, home equity can be likened to a bank deposit, increasing in value and available for use if needed.

Because lenders realize that loans secured by homes are safe investments for them, rates for home equity loans are significantly less than for personal property or business loans. Lenders know that homes are unlikely to suffer any significant reduction in value.

DEDUCTIBILITY OF TAXES AND INTEREST

Under the Tax Reform Act of 1986, many special tax considerations and deductions have been eliminated. But a tax deduction that was left largely unchanged is the interest deduction on financing for home ownership. Specifically:

- Taxes on real or tangible property are deductible.
- Interest on a home equity or second-mortgage loan is deductible when you use the money for home improvements, but the law limits interest deductions to $100,000 of home-equity borrowing when you use the money for any other purpose.

As an additional benefit, the preceding deductions are generally available for purposes of state income taxes as well as for federal taxes.

To understand the value of these deductions, assume a homeowner is paying $1,000 a month on a home loan. At least $900 of this payment would likely represent interest and property taxes. Further assuming a combined federal and state tax rate of 30 percent, the homeowner would enjoy a tax savings of $270 ($900 × .30). Thus, the net cost to the homeowner would be just $730 a month. On the other hand, a person who makes a rent payment of $1,000 each month obtains no tax benefits. The $1,000 must be paid out of fully taxable income.

Tax reform has made home ownership more attractive than ever; it represents one of the few remaining tax advantages available to the average consumer.

$125,000 TAX EXCLUSION

A very important tax exclusion was not affected by the Tax Reform Act of 1986. A taxpayer age 55 or older can exclude from income up to $125,000 from the gain realized on the sale of the taxpayer's principal residence. The taxpayer must have lived in the home for three of the five years preceeding the sale. In the case of joint ownership, only one spouse need be 55 years of age or older. Compare this with an investment that does not have this exclusion: Assuming a 28 percent tax bracket, taxes payable on $125,000 amount to $35,000. The federal government thus allows you to realize and keep, tax free, the appreciation in the value of your home up to $125,000. Many states offer similar homeowner exclusions.

A point to keep in mind is that the $125,000 exclusion is a one-time-only option. If one spouse participated in this one-time exclusion during a previous marriage, the exclusion would not be available to the other spouse if the property is jointly owned.

TAX-DEFERRED SALE

Also left unchanged by the 1986 Tax Reform Act was the ability to defer paying taxes on profit from the sale of a residence. If, within two years of selling a home, the owner purchases another residence that costs the same or more than the selling price of the previous home, no income taxes are due on the profit from the sale. If a new home is not purchased within two years, then the profit would be taxable. However, by waiting until age 55 to sell, the owner can take advantage of the $125,000 exclusion, not replace the home, and still avoid paying the tax.

A homeowner can sell his residence, in which he may have considerable equity, for cash, and then buy another home with a low down payment. In this way, the homeowner could end up with a great deal of cash and no taxes to pay on the gain from the home sale.

INCOME CONSIDERATIONS

A home is a desirable commodity; people are willing to pay rent for the use of this commodity. To provide income, homes can be rented on an annual basis, or they can be rented seasonally or when not required by the owner. Parts of homes or ancillary buildings on the property can also be rented. In many cities, garages rent for over $100 per month. Many people rent just a single room; others share a home with another person. For elderly homeowners, offering housing in return for care has served as an attractive alternative to the necessity of a nursing home.

RENTAL CONVERSIONS

Where zoning allows conversion, many owners have found that it makes economic sense to convert basement, attic, or even garage space to a rental apartment. Funds for the conversion can be obtained by a home improvement loan and payments made from the rent receipts. In this way, not only is income possible, but the improvement can increase the property's value, and thus the owner's equity, as well.

Chapter 2:
Which Type of Home
Is For You?

What a person needs and what a person wants are two entirely different things. Your housing needs are to meet basic shelter requirements. Your wants, on the other hand, go far beyond your needs.

A PRACTICAL APPROACH

Unless you have a custom home designed and built for you and can do so without budgetary restraints, don't expect to find a home that meets all of your wants. Your wants could include location, size, number of bedrooms and baths, lot size, architectural style, built-in features, garage size, room arrangement, orientation to the sun, and even decor. To be realistic, your wants must be in line with your ability to finance and pay for them. Otherwise, your wants are likely to remain unfulfilled wishes.

Since it's unlikely that you would find a home that meets all your requirements, consider prioritizing your wants under three categories:

• Must Have
• Strongly Desire
• Would Like

Separately, your spouse should prepare a similar list, and then you can compare and complete a final categorized want list.

If residency in a particular community is a job requirement, then location would be a "must have." If a family wanted four bedrooms but would accept three if they were large, four bedrooms would be a "strongly desire" want. For a family with small children, a fenced yard or the ability to fence the yard would likely be a "must have" feature.

Generally, features that homebuyers list as "must have" are not all present in the home they finally purchase. The reason "must have" features are forgotten is that other features tend to outweigh the absence of what was once considered a "must." The "must" feature often turns out to be only "strongly desired." By limiting your home's "must" features to those that are really your minimum acceptable features, you will have a great many more homes to choose from. Obviously, then, this increases the likelihood that you will find a home on the market that best meets your needs and desires.

ARCHITECTURAL STYLE

Most people want their homes to reflect their personality or how they view themselves or want others to view them. Some home designs are imaginative; others are staid copies of the types of homes built long ago. Some homes are bright and showy, and others seem to blend unobtrusively into their surroundings. When considering a home purchase, keep in mind that it is *you* and no one else who must be pleased with the house—that is, until it's time to sell.

While many people love to look at homes that are architecturally novel, even radical, it is the rare person who would personally want to own such a home. The majority of buyers prefer traditional housing. There is a ready market for English Tudor, French Norman, Georgian, New England Colonial, Cape Cod, Italian Renaissance, Spanish Colonial, California Ranch, and other traditional home styles.

If you choose to build a home that is architecturally unusual, don't build it with the expectation of financial profit. Consider your profit to be in the enjoyment of living in the home. If you want something truly novel, it's best to look for an unusual home built for another owner who now wishes to sell. Because you will be one of only a few interested buyers, you may be able to realize a significant savings above and beyond what it would cost you to reproduce that home yourself.

OLDER HOMES

While many people concentrate their househunting efforts on newer housing, older homes do offer a number of advantages. They offer neighborhoods where the character has been established. Improvements such as paved streets, curbs, gutters, sidewalks, and sewer and water lines have likely been installed and already paid for. This reduces the likelihood of receiving special tax assessments. Older homes often offer distinction and workmanship seldom found in new homes. They may also offer the very important benefit of more space for the money.

Many older homes were built to a level of quality evident today in only the most expensive of new homes. Woodwork and trim in many older homes is elaborate. A great many people have recently discovered that new isn't necessarily better and now relish the individuality and classic beauty of an older home. And, as any decorator will tell you, older homes are better suited than new homes for period furniture.

Because older homes are often owned free and clear by present owners, attractive owner financing may be available. This benefit is of greater importance in tight money markets.

On the other hand, older homes require greater attention than new homes. The owner of an older home should either be able to handle a succession of minor repairs, or be willing to hire others to make the repairs. Remember that bringing in contractors for every minor repair and/or improvement can be very expensive.

Other disadvantages of older homes can include deteriorating plumbing, inadequate wiring, inefficient heating and cooling, inadequate insulation, and so on. Some older homes have serious structural damage resulting from age, rot, and/or termites. A physical inspection by an expert, as discussed in Chapter 6, is very important prior to the purchase of an older home.

NEW HOMES

New homes offer the homeowner both advantages and disadvantages.

New homes often come with a builder warranty, but many owners find that getting a builder to return for minor work can be very frustrating. Also, though major structural repairs are fewer in a new home, there usually is far more *immediate* work for the homeowner that involves great expense: Landscaping, walks, patios, fences, shelving, draperies and rods are some things to consider.

On the positive side, because of better insulation and modern heating and cooling units, new homes generally are far more energy-efficient than older homes. The result is lower heating and cooling costs.

When buying a home from a model, you should find out exactly what is and what is not in the basic house. Too often, features that homebuyers thought were included in the purchase price (such as a dishwasher or drapes) turn out to be extras or decorator items. A good idea is to add the following to your purchase contract: "Home to be completed in the same manner and quality as the model located at _____ with the exception of _____."

By asking for such a clause, you will quickly discover which features are not standard.

When considering a home in a new subdivision, you should ascertain which improvements will be included and paid for by the developer. In some developments, the improvements are bonded and the homeowner must pay for them with annual tax payments or assessments. This results in a higher price for the property.

If the home has a septic system and/or private well, you should determine the likelihood of city services being installed in the foreseeable future. While city water and sewer are generally positive features that add to the property value, they will also result in additional expense.

CONVENTIONAL CONSTRUCTION

Most housing is *conventionally* or *stick-built*. While some factory-assembled components such as cabinets and trusses are commonly used, most of the house is completed on site. Conventionally constructed housing generally offers the greatest resale value.

PREFABRICATED HOUSING

Prefabricated homes are completed on site from factory-assembled components. The degree of factory and site work varies greatly by manufacturer. Many homes are built in 8-foot to 16-foot wall, ceiling, and floor sections, and are unloaded by cranes at the site and bolted together. Some homes have completed plumbing cores ready to be hooked to city services. Many are factory wired. A large percentage of prefabricated homes built today are of excellent quality, although some are not. For example, some manufacturers use lightweight interior partitions that allow considerable noise transmission from room to room.

The primary advantages of prefabrication are savings of time and money. A prefabricated home can be completed in days, while building conventional housing can take months. Therefore, financing costs are materially decreased. The construction costs per square foot for prefabricated housing are considerably less than the construction costs per square foot of similar-quality conventional housing. The reason for the lower cost is that factory work involves mass production, which is almost always cheaper. There are no weather delays or waiting time for other trades or materials. Bulk purchases reduce material costs, and factory work done to specified plans reduces waste. In addition, on-site vandalism and theft are practically eliminated.

In many areas of the country, prefabrication has met stiff resistance from both unions and community building agencies. The differences in code requirements between communities have also hindered prefabrication.

While prefabrication can offer more house for the money, the negative side is that resale values are likely to be less than if the housing were conventionally built.

MODULAR HOUSING

A *modular house* is a factory-built home that is simply moved to the site in several sections and assembled. It differs from a prefabricated house in the degree of factory assembling and differs from a mobile home in that it is not built on its own chassis. It must be transported by truck.

Modular housing offers cost advantages for the same reasons that prefabrication saves money. Because of time and investment savings, modular housing provides an attractive option for vacation homes. But modular housing has the disadvantage of a lower resale value than conventional housing.

MOBILE HOMES

The *mobile homes* of today evolved from the gypsy wagons of Europe, our own Conestoga wagons, and our early travel trailers. Today's mobile homes are not truly mobile at all. While they are transported to their site on wheels attached to a chassis or frame, once set up, they are seldom moved. It is estimated that fewer than 10 percent of mobile homes are again moved to be used as housing units after they have been placed on site.

Mobile homes in "own your own lot" parks are more likely to show significant appreciation in value than homes in rental parks. This is due primarily to increase in site value. While units in some desirable rental parks have shown appreciation, mobile homes in general experience far less appreciation than conventional housing. It is not unusual for the value of mobile homes to depreciate despite a general real estate inflation. The positive aspect of this is that depreciation has created excellent purchase opportunities of some older units.

Financing costs of mobile home purchases can be a drawback. These costs are generally 1 to 2 percent higher than for conventional-home financing because of increased risk to the lender. Historically, mobile homes have not appreciated in value as much as conventional housing, and their relative repossession value is much lower. On the positive side, many dealers arrange low down payment financing that includes installation, furniture, and appliances.

KIT HOMES

In 1908, Sears started selling mail-order or *kit homes*. The material was precut and included everything but the home's foundation. By the time Sears discontinued selling their homes in 1937, more than 100,000 of them had been erected. The styles ranged from modest bungalows and privies to elaborate antebellum mansions. The buyers received detailed instructions, and either built the homes themselves or hired contractors.

Precut home packages are still available, generally on a regional basis. Many large lumber companies offer these packaged home kits. Specialty packages for log houses and geodesic domes are also available.

The appeal of a kit home is the substantial savings that are possible as well as the tremendous pride an owner achieves in having built his or her own home. People who have built kit homes typically have an excellent feeling about their homes.

A disadvantage of kit homes is that the site must be purchased separately. Another disadvantage is financing. Many lenders are reluctant to make home loans to owner-builders who lack proven construction experience. The sellers of some of these kit homes do, however, provide financing for owner-builders. Some sellers also provide expert technical help for owner-builders.

SHELL HOMES

A *shell home* is a foundation and a (usually) completed exterior. Typically, the interior is just studded in with rough flooring. Designed for completion by the owner, shell homes are often sold as vacation homes that include a lot and a developer-financing package. Owners often camp in the house and complete construction while living in it. The sellers usually include detailed plans for completion as well as a list of contractors and prices for various work that the homeowner may wish to contract.

CONDOMINIUMS, PLANNED UNIT DEVELOPMENTS, AND COOPERATIVES

A *condominium* involves separate ownership of a housing unit, but common ownership of the land and common areas (such as a pool or recreation building) with the other owners. Condominiums are often referred to as *vertical subdivisions*. Typically, the owner of a condominium unit owns the space that extends to the interior of the exterior walls, floor, and ceiling. The exterior walls are generally part of the common area. Condominium dwellings often are converted apartment buildings; newer condominiums are frequently constructed in the *single-family attached housing* style, often as so-called *carriage homes* or *townhouses*.

Maintenance and insurance of a condominium's common area are covered by a condominium fee that is assessed on a monthly basis. Condominium fees vary greatly; be sure to ascertain these costs before making a condominium purchase.

A *planned unit development* (PUD), though similar to a condominium in that certain areas are owned in common, differs because each owner owns the land beneath his or her unit.

In a *cooperative*, a corporation takes title to the property. Each owner owns a share of stock in the corporation and has the right to occupy a unit under a lease with the corporation. In some cooperatives, lease transfers are subject to approval by a board of directors.

Advantages

Besides the freedom from maintenance that they provide, a major advantage of condominiums, planned unit developments, and cooperatives is a lower price per unit than for a similarly located single-family home. Increased tenant density allows for this price break.

Many apartments have been converted to condominiums and cooperatives. In addition, condominiums and cooperatives have been overbuilt in many areas of the country. The result is a supply that exceeds present demand, and thus creates exceptional purchase opportunities.

Disadvantages

Disadvantages of condominiums and cooperative ownership are similar to those associated with apartment living, chiefly noise and lack of privacy. Additionally, condominiums and cooperatives generally have extensive restrictions on use. Before purchase of any unit, review these restrictions. As an example, pets over a certain size or weight may be prohibited. The hours during which common areas may be used may be strictly governed, and there will likely be limitations on guests and such things as musical instruments, stereos, and water beds. If you don't like apartment life, don't be too quick to buy a condominium or cooperative.

CONTRACTING TO BUILD

When you contract with a builder to construct a new home for you, you enter into a relationship that has both advantages and disadvantages. On the plus side, you'll be able to get the site you want, and can specify design materials and colors the way you want them. Cost savings are also possible. When a builder constructs a house for speculation (that is, with the hope that the home will be purchased after completion), he adds to the price his own interest costs and the cost of holding the property for resale. A "spec" (speculative) builder also expects a greater profit margin for the additional risk involved. On the other hand, when the builder builds under contract, risks are reduced. Interest costs are borne by the buyer's construction loan. A savings of 10 percent should be possible between a speculative home a builder has for sale and a similar home you wish the builder to construct for you under contract.

Disadvantages of contracting a home include unexpected problems, delays, and aggravation. Many builders anticipate that you will want changes once construction begins. They will demand a markup for these changes in order to increase their overall profit. In other cases, where the builder is on shaky financial ground, work on the home can come to a startling, sudden halt. It's wise to have your lender check the builder's credit history before you contract for construction. Lawsuits between contractors and homebuyers sometimes occur. Typically, these suits arise due to poor communication or agreements made verbally between the builder and the customer. A word to the wise: Any agreement between a homebuyer and a builder should be clearly expressed in writing, and should include a thorough accounting of schedules and materials.

Construction Costs

For greater value per dollar, consider a two-story home. Two-story homes offer double the square footage of one-story homes that have comparable roofs and foundations. The price per square foot for two-story homes is therefore less than the price per square foot of one-story homes of similar quality.

A raised ranch offers an even lower price per square foot. By building the first-level "basement" about four feet above the ground, window space is available so that the basement can be fully utilized for living space.

On sloping lots, the basement can be utilized for living space by adding windows. Lots that slope up from a road allow for a garage at the basement level, which can mean a significant savings over the cost of an attached garage.

When evaluating the plans of new homes, keep in mind that the number of feet of exterior wall and foundation is an important cost consideration. For example, a rectangular home 32 feet by 40 feet contains 1,280 square feet and has 144 linear feet of exterior wall. A 24-foot by 53-foot home has 1,272 square feet, and is more expensive to build, having 154 linear feet of wall and foundation. Jogs in the walls may enhance the appearance, but you should understand that they also increase costs.

There are savings of scale when you build bigger. When dealing with similar-quality housing, a larger home costs less per square foot to construct than does a smaller home. As an example, a 4,000-square foot home would not cost twice as much to build as a 2,000-square foot home. In doubling the size, the exterior walls are not doubled, nor is the cost of lot preparation, sewer connection, or the like. The house still has only one kitchen. Electrical, plumbing, heating, and cooling costs would be unlikely to double with a doubling of the size. Therefore, a flat construction price per square foot for housing is likely to be a bargain for smaller homes, but excessive for larger homes.

Chapter 3:
How Much Can You Afford?

Of primary concern to most people who are in the market for a home is how much they can afford to pay. What you can afford to pay for housing is based on several factors:

- The amount of your down payment
- The interest rates on home loans at the time of purchase
- Your current income and expenses
- Your priorities

DOWN PAYMENT

How much you apply as a *down payment* on a home will determine the amount you will need to finance. The amount you finance, in turn, will determine your monthly payments.

There are a variety of sources available to you for a home down payment. Obviously, your savings are an immediate source of cash. In addition to your savings, you should consider your life insurance. While term insurance has no loan value, most other life insurance policies provide for policy loans. Interest rates on these loans are generally far below market interest rates, but are no longer tax-deductible.

Family, friends, and loan companies are additional sources for home down payments. However, borrowing should only be done if you are willing and able to make the necessary sacrifices to honor your repayment agreement. Remember that a mortgage lender will count a down-payment loan as an outstanding obligation when you apply for a mortgage loan.

Use of credit cards for a down payment is a technique sometimes recommended by presenters of real estate seminars. Besides the fact that many lenders will not even allow such a down payment, credit card use for this purpose should be avoided because of the extremely high interest rate, the lack of deductibility from state or federal taxes, and the relatively short repayment schedule.

When considering your available down payment amount, keep in mind that you'll want to retain some money as a reserve. You will have to pay a variety of *closing costs* when you take possession of the home (as discussed in Chapter 8), and will likely have move-in expenses that you did not contemplate. For emergencies, financial planners recommend that you have liquid reserves (money or securities readily convertible to cash) equal to between two and three months' of your income.

The stability of your present income will affect how much you should keep in reserve. Greater stability, represented by a stable, secure job, would indicate that reserves could be lessened. If, however, you were a commission salesperson in an industry that had experienced cycles of good and bad times, greater personal reserves than otherwise indicated should be considered. Keep in mind that there are methods of financing a home that do not require large down payments (see Chapter 7).

INTEREST RATES

Interest rates are another important factor in determining the amount you can afford to pay for a home, since interest is assessed monthly on the amount you finance or borrow. The 1980s have seen generally lower interest rates.

Reproduced on page 22 are sample loan amortization tables. *Amortization* is the reduction of debt by regular payments of interest and principal sufficient to pay off a loan by maturity. The tables—the first

15-YEAR AMORTIZATION TABLE

Monthly Payments

Amount	10%	10½%	11%	11½%	12%
$50,000	$537.50	$553.00	$568.50	$584.50	$600.50
60,000	645.00	663.60	682.20	701.40	720.60
70,000	752.50	774.20	795.90	818.30	840.70
80,000	860.00	884.80	909.60	935.20	960.80
90,000	967.50	995.40	1,023.30	1,052.10	1,080.90
100,000	1,075.00	1,106.00	1,137.00	1,169.00	1,201.00
110,000	1,182.50	1,216.60	1,250.70	1,285.90	1,321.10
120,000	1,290.00	1,327.20	1,364.40	1,402.80	1,441.20
130,000	1,397.50	1,437.80	1,478.10	1,519.70	1,561.30
140,000	1,505.00	1,548.40	1,591.80	1,636.60	1,681.40
150,000	1,612.50	1,659.00	1,705.50	1,753.50	1,801.50

30-YEAR AMORTIZATION TABLE

Monthly Payments

Amount	10%	10½%	11%	11½%	12%
$50,000	$439.00	$457.50	$476.50	$495.00	$514.50
60,000	526.80	549.00	571.80	594.60	617.40
70,000	614.60	640.50	667.10	693.70	720.30
80,000	702.40	732.00	762.40	792.80	823.20
90,000	790.20	823.50	857.70	891.90	926.10
100,000	878.00	915.00	953.00	991.00	1,029.00
110,000	965.80	1,006.50	1,048.30	1,090.10	1,131.90
120,000	1,053.60	1,098.00	1,143.60	1,189.20	1,234.80
130,000	1,141.40	1,189.50	1,238.90	1,288.30	1,337.70
140,000	1,229.20	1,281.00	1,334.20	1,387.40	1,440.60
150,000	1,317.00	1,372.50	1,429.50	1,486.50	1,543.50

assuming a 15-year loan, the second assuming a 30-year loan—show the monthly payments necessary to pay off loans in amounts ranging from $50,000 to $150,000, at interest rates ranging from 10 percent to 12 percent. The monthly payment figures shown on the charts do not include such expenses as insurance and property taxes. For more information about amortization periods, see Chapter 7.

YOUR INCOME AND EXPENSES

While most people have a good understanding of the amount of income they receive, they have a poor grasp as to where their money goes. By understanding what happens to your money after you receive it, you can determine what money is available for housing, while accounting for current spending habits. Because home buying often requires reallocation of resources, an analysis of how you spend your money will provide you with information as to the maximum amount you can or are willing to allocate for housing.

The sample worksheet on page 24 will help you figure, in dollars and cents, what your home payment ability is.

When determining your monthly income, do not include overtime pay because this income can be easily terminated. You should consider second-job income only if you have a history of working a second job and/or feel that you can continue the effort.

Don't include income from deposits or investments if those funds will be used for your down payment. For royalty and stock income, do not count on more than two-thirds of current income, because of possible market fluctuations.

To arrive at your monthly expense figures, it is recommended you check your credit card purchase billings and your check stubs and try to arrive at monthly averages. Your total expenses plus savings should equal your income. If expenses exceed your

Monthly Expenses

	Current	Revised
Rent (or house payment):	_____	_____
Car Payment:	_____	_____
Insurance	_____	_____
Auto:	_____	_____
Life:	_____	_____
Property:	_____	_____
Health:	_____	_____
Groceries and		
Household Supplies:	_____	_____
Gas and Oil:	_____	_____
Automobile Maintenance:	_____	_____
Entertainment:	_____	_____
Utilities:	_____	_____
Clothing:	_____	_____
Credit Card Payments:	_____	_____
Loan Payments:	_____	_____
Charitable Contributions:	_____	_____
Education/Tuition:	_____	_____
Other:	_____	_____
Savings:	_____	_____
Miscellaneous:	_____	_____
Totals	$_____	$_____

Monthly Income
  (Net Received)   **Total** $_____

income, you are deficit spending, and a rearrangement of your budget is necessary. If some adjustment is required, try to be realistic in the adjustments you make.

The amount available for home payments, currently or even with the revised budget, might still be insufficient to finance the housing you want, based on current interest rates and the amount you need to finance. Should this be the case, there are a number of solutions:

- *Lower your housing aspirations*. Purchase a starter home to obtain the equity necessary so you can eventually move up to the type of housing you desire.
- *Obtain a lower-interest-rate loan* (see Chapter 7).
- *Increase your income through a part-time job or employment for a nonworking spouse.*
- *Reallocate your resources*. For example, plan to spend less on entertainment, clothing, and travel, and divert those dollars saved toward the mortgage payment.

Most homebuyers who find their income insufficient to meet their housing wants have used a combination of the above. The last solution, however, is generally the most effective one.

YOUR PRIORITIES

Adjusting your priorities involves rethinking or redefining what is important to you. For instance, many young families own two expensive cars. Their car payments and insurance add up to a significant monthly expense. Often the only way such a family can become homeowners is to sacrifice one or both cars in favor of less expensive or older models.

As you look at homes and as you drive through different neighborhoods, you will see newer model Cadillacs, Mercedes, and expensive recreational vehicles parked in front of relatively modest housing. You will also see older economy cars in garages and carports of far more expensive homes. What you are really seeing is the priority of individual homeowners, and the standards they've set for themselves. If a home is of greater importance to you, the expensive car might have to go. But keep in mind that although you might have to forego restaurant lunches in favor of a brown bag, this is likely to be only a temporary cutback. Giving up something to become a homeowner does not mean giving it up for good. Locking in your house payments now will result in more spendable money in the future.

Most potential homeowners have heard these two rules of thumb: A home should cost no more than two and a half times gross income, and payments should not exceed 25 to 28 percent of gross income. These rules are useful, but are only general guidelines. Besides the requirements of your lender, the amount you can afford is determined by your priorities, and not by generalities.

Personal priorities with regard to what housing a family can afford vary greatly. We know that as a general rule, white-collar workers are willing to spend a greater percentage of their incomes for housing than are blue-collar workers in similar income brackets. Similarly, studies have shown that highly educated people tend to spend more for housing than less-educated people who have similar incomes.

In Orange County, California, where housing costs are among the highest in the nation, it is common for families to spend 50 percent of their income for housing. Patterns in other parts of the country are different.

When assessing your financial position and determining what you can afford to pay, keep in mind that most families who set a payment limit end up exceeding that limit. Nevertheless, on a national basis, fewer than two percent of home mortgages end in foreclosure. People tend to do what they have to in order to buy and keep a home.

For young professionals with escalating incomes, or for anyone who anticipates significant increases in income, it might be wise to buy a home now that you will be happy with in the future. Sacrifices are likely to be short-lived. Also, as you will see in Chapter 7, mortgages can be tailored to the needs of such purchasers with lower payments during the first few years.

Simply because you are willing to make sacrifices in order to make a required loan payment does not mean you can qualify for a loan. Lenders tend to use strict formulas based on your earnings. As the money supply tightens, lenders become more conservative and accordingly tighten their lending requirements. But just because a lender indicates that the highest loan you can qualify for is less than you want does not mean you will have to settle for lower-quality housing. Chapter 7 explains financing techniques that will allow you to meet your wants.

OTHER HOME EXPENSES

A mortgage payment for principal and interest is not the only expense of home ownership. You will likely be faced with the following additional expenses:

- *Property taxes.* Taxes are assessed against the value of property; they do vary by area. A local real estate agent can give you a good idea what to expect in taxes. What a current owner pays for property taxes may be less than what you as the potential buyer of that property would pay because in many areas property is reassessed upon sale.

- *Insurance.* Your lender will probably require insurance for the loan amount as a condition of the financing agreement, even if a great part of the property's value is in the land. When you shop around, you will find that rates between insurers vary a great deal. You might also want mortgage insurance, which is a form of term life insurance that pays off the loan in the event of death or permanent disability.

- *Utilities.* Even though you may have paid utilities in an apartment, utility costs for a home will be significantly greater. If you're contemplating the purchase of a home that's currently occupied, ask the existing owners what kind of utility payments they make or ask to see their utility bills for the past year. If you're interested in a new home, check with the people who live in the neighborhood. Heating and/or cooling costs can be substantial. And don't forget water bills. Renters rarely pay for water costs, and it's an expense many tend to overlook when they buy their own homes. Once you're a homeowner, water bills are your responsibility; in many areas of the country, water is a major expenditure.

- *Maintenance and repair.* Garden tools, seed, fertilizer, hardware, paint, and the like are expenses to be considered. Additionally, if you cannot make plumbing and electrical repairs yourself, the costs could be significant, especially for older homes.
- *Other expenses.* Depending on the home and area, other expenses to consider would be garbage and trash removal, cable television, pest control service, water softener, owner association dues, and special assessments. If the home you're interested in has a pool, there will be a high water usage and chemical costs if a pool service is not used.

A WORD OF ADVICE

As a final word, do not make the mistake of committing yourself and/or your family to a monthly home payment that exceeds your ability—or your willingness—to pay. While some sacrifice may be necessary, the prospect of never having enough money to enjoy an occasional luxury or a normal social life can put an extreme strain on you and your family. Remember your priorities: Your emotional well-being and that of your family should be at the top of your list.

Chapter 4:
Location

You've heard it many times: The three most important factors that determine a home's value are location, location, and location. It's true. And while location is a prime determinant of value for all real estate, it is of particular importance when the property is a single-family home.

As a general rule, you should look for a home that meets your needs in the best neighborhood you can afford. Such a home can be expected to realize the greatest appreciation. In the long run, bargain-priced homes in less desirable neighborhoods are often not bargains at all. The homeowner who might have even overpaid at the time of purchase for a home in a prime neighborhood might find that the property was a true bargain when it comes time to sell.

FINDING AREAS TO EVALUATE

A good area map provides an excellent starting point to check and evaluate particular neighborhoods. Sunday drives through various neighborhoods, accompanied by open house visits, will give you a feel for value of homes in a given area.

If you are interested in a particular area or areas, stop and ask questions of people you see working in their front yards. People will generally be very helpful if you indicate that you are interested in locating in their neighborhood. Ask questions about commuting time, the quality and location of schools, recreational facilities, shopping, churches, medical facilities, taxes, costs of services and utilities, problems in the area, and other basic concerns.

If you belong to an organized faith, contact the neighborhood minister, priest, or rabbi, who should be able to answer most questions you have, or could refer you to someone who can. The local Chamber of Commerce is another excellent source of information.

NEIGHBORHOOD ANALYSIS

By definition, a neighborhood is an area of social conformity. Neighborhoods might have defined physical boundaries such as school districts. Some subdivisions become distinct neighborhoods. Others are less definable, with one neighborhood melding into the next.

Homogeneous neighborhoods of people having similar social and economic backgrounds tend to be stable; homes are usually well maintained and there exists a feeling of neighborhood pride. Such strong neighborhoods mean that home values are likely to be maintained.

Age Factor

A neighborhood of younger white-collar and professional workers with young children is likely to be a desirable neighborhood for many years. Children help the cohesiveness of a neighborhood. Local activities in which neighbors can join together, such as scouting, little league, or school functions, result in close interaction and a strong neighborhood interest. Such a neighborhood is highly desired by others of similar interests.

As a neighborhood ages, and its children leave, it tends to lose its cohesiveness. The graying of a neighborhood generally results in a greater property turnover. Couples whose children have grown and moved and who own homes that are now too large, or owners who wish to retire to other areas will put their homes on the market. Homeowners who are either unable to sell or who want income will rent their homes. Others will rent rooms they no longer need.

The result is a neighborhood population that may be transitory. Such a neighborhood usually should be avoided because it is poised for what could be a rapid decline. An increase of renters and/or roomers in a neighborhood is sometimes an early indicator of trouble ahead.

Renters

Renters in a single-family home often do not have the same pride as owners. They seldom maintain their rented property as an owner would. Renters often fail to perform what would be considered minimum maintenance.

Public Housing

Public housing projects established in or near a neighborhood, while serving a community need, can be expected to have a negative effect on property values. This is due to the increase in the number of young people, some of whom may belong to gangs that intimidate area residents. Crime rates near public housing are often higher than in other areas.

Graffiti

The presence of graffiti on walls is a strong negative indicator with regard to a neighborhood's desirability. It points to the presence of youth gangs, as well as to feelings of hopelessness or indifference on the part of property owners who fail to remove the markings. Such neighborhoods may deteriorate further.

Turnaround Areas

While it is best to avoid areas that seem to be poised for a decline, you should be aware that many formerly undesirable neighborhoods close to central cities are making dramatic turnarounds.

As examples, older Victorian homes in many cities are being sought by young professionals who appreciate the homes' charm and beauty. Row houses, once rented to the poor, are being completely renovated by owners in upper-income brackets. In many cities, areas that were once regarded as slums are now considered highly fashionable.

Areas that are likely to turn around are those close to central office districts, preferably within walking distance. Distinctive architecture is a big plus. Other positive signs to look for are recent sales to people with higher incomes and/or education than most of the existing residents. A turnaround may be indicated by the renovation of several homes in the same block.

An advantage of buying turnaround property is that structurally sound buildings may be purchased for much less than if they were located in other, more desirable areas. Turnaround neighborhoods also offer the benefits of short commutes and proximity to the city's culture, entertainment, and restaurants.

Progression and Regression

In every large city you will find homes that would be highly desirable and command much higher sales prices if they were located in better neighborhoods. As a corollary, you will also see small, nondescript homes that demand high selling prices because they are located in good neighborhoods of finer homes. What you are seeing is the application of the principles of *progression* and *regression*.

The *principle of progression* is that an area's more desirable or expensive homes tend to increase the desirability and thus the value of less opulent homes in the area.

The *principle of regression* is that less desirable property use and/or housing in a specific area will decrease the value of more expensive homes.

A low-quality or neglected home next to a more expensive home will negatively affect the value of the better home.

The principle of regression can even apply to beauty. An unprepossessing home would negatively affect the value of more attractive homes around it.

If you are considering a home in a new subdivision, know that the least expensive home is likely to experience the highest percentage of value increase, while the highest-priced home might experience the lowest increase. While the higher-priced homes tend to elevate the value of the lowest-priced homes, the lowest-priced homes would tend to decrease the value of the highest-price homes.

The principles of progression and regression can apply to entire neighborhoods. A very expensive residential development would have a positive effect on an adjoining neighborhood, but a low-cost or rental project would have a negative effect on neighborhood values.

Conformity

The *principle of conformity* is that value is most likely to be maintained in an area of similar use. For example, a house in the center of a single-family residential development would likely have a higher value than one located on the edge of a development that adjoins apartments or commercial buildings.

Desirable Areas

Areas likely to show exceptional appreciation are those in close proximity to proposed golf courses, colleges, and public schools. For retirement areas, developments close to medical centers are particularly likely to become highly desirable.

Zoning

All residential zoning and code enforcement (local laws that regulate the commercial and residential use of land) is not the same. In areas with tight zoning control and enforcement, property values are likely to appreciate much more significantly than in areas where enforcement is not as strong. Thus, zoning and code enforcement work to maintain values. Economically, it would be in your best interest to locate in a community of strong codes.

Areas of zoning change in which less desirable uses or conversion of uses are being approved should be avoided. While the change in zoning from residential to commercial could result in greatly increased property values, it is more likely that your home would remain residentially zoned in an area having an undesirable mix of residential and commercial use. Such an area would have an increase in the number of renters, noise, and traffic, and could be expected to decline in value.

Restricted Covenants

In addition to zoning, which is a public restriction, many communities have adopted *restrictive covenants*, which are private restrictions. Also known as "covenants, conditions, and restrictions" (CC & R's), restrictive covenants are agreements by the homeowners to be bound by a set of rules that are generally much more restrictive than zoning. For example, restrictive covenants could prohibit recreational vehicles in driveways, or auto repair in driveways. They could require green lawns or prohibit storage sheds. The purpose of these restrictions is to maintain the character and value of a subdivision. In subdivisions with strong neighborhood associations, these restrictions are often strictly enforced. While you might not agree with some of the restrictions, an area that adopts them and strongly enforces them will more likely retain its desirability than areas with less stringent restrictions and/or enforcement.

Commercial Analysis

Neighborhood shopping areas are another important element and should be studied carefully when analyzing a neighborhood. A low vacancy rate for commercial stores, quality stores, and businesses that have been at their present location for a number of years is a positive factor. Conversely, a high vacancy rate, or a high business turnover rate is a negative factor, indicating a less than stable neighborhood. Also to be avoided are areas that cater to undesirable elements with unsavory businesses, such as rowdy taverns and "adult" book stores.

The absence of shopping in a newly developed area is not really a negative factor. Commercial development can generally be expected to follow residential growth.

Building Restrictions

Many communities today are attempting to limit or stop future growth. The reason may be the inability of the community to service uncontrolled growth or a desire to maintain a less crowded, less frenetic way of life. Areas that have or are likely to have growth limitations and/or moratoriums should be considered. The net effect of reducing future growth will be to limit the supply of housing. And thus, the market forces of supply and demand can be expected to pull prices up.

Streets

While you may want to be near a major traffic thoroughfare or expressway, you don't want to be right on it or too close to it. Noise and noise vibration, fumes, and traffic would make living conditions far less desirable than you would have with a home situated several blocks away.

Generally, a site on a one-way street (where easy access is limited) is not as desirable as a site on a street that carries two-way traffic. On the other hand, property on a cul-de-sac (dead end street) is highly desirable because of the limited traffic.

Lots

Generally, sites with oddly shaped lots such as triangles are not as desirable as those with standard rectangular lots. A wide, shallow site is generally more desirable than a narrow, deep lot since it is conducive to wide ranch homes. When it comes time to sell, know that purchasers are attracted to homes that look impressive from the street. Without curb appeal, many people will not leave their cars to inspect a home.

Lot size is important to many purchasers. The fact that there is room to store a recreational vehicle in the yard or room for a large garden or children's play area is important. Unusually small sites should be avoided primarily because they will make resale difficult.

COMMUTING

If you find that the housing within desirable areas is beyond your financial ability, consider expanding your search, even though it will increase commuting time and distance. For example, because of high land costs in Orange County, California, thousands of people now commute to their jobs from new developments in the Riverside area, where housing costs can be as low as half of those in Orange County. These buyers are willing to commute in order to have the home and lifestyle that they desire.

EXURBIA

Exurbia is the area beyond the suburbs. It is characterized by farms and scattered housing clusters, as well as isolated homes and small towns. Many homebuyers are deciding that exurbia is the place to go. Advantages include significantly lower housing costs, larger housing sites, generally lower costs for services, and—most important to many buyers—a quiet lifestyle. Chief disadvantages of exurban living are long daily commutes and remoteness from urban and suburban shopping, culture, and entertainment.

Chapter 5:
Finding Your Home

SERIOUS HOUSE HUNTING

A home will likely be the largest single investment of your life. You will probably live in your home for many years. Once you make a purchase, you will be locked into a particular piece of property. Therefore, the importance of location cannot be overemphasized. After you have taken the time to select the general location that appeals to you, you'll be ready for the next step on the road to home ownership: serious house hunting.

MARKET VALUE

The accepted method for appraising or determining the market value of single-family residences is called the "market comparison approach." The appraiser looks for recent sales of equally desirable properties sold by willing sellers to willing buyers. Because houses have differing locations and amenities, the appraiser must balance these variables. For example, the appraiser might decide that an 1,800-square foot 2½-bath home that is 15 years old is worth the same as an 18-year-old home of similar construction having 1,950 square feet and two baths. An appraiser might determine that because of a prime view, one house is worth $15,000 more than a similar home in the same area.

By actively house hunting, you are really doing the same thing that an appraiser does. You, however, base your conclusions on asking or list prices, not sale prices. If you determine that the asking price of a given home is too high, what you really mean is that the price is too high in comparison with the prices being asked for similarly desirable homes. Unconsciously, you are balancing out the amenities of the homes. When you finally do buy a home, you will be applying the *principle of substitution*, meaning that you will not pay more for one home than the amount you would have to pay for another, equally desirable home.

A questionable technique used by some agents, when a prospect is unfamiliar with an area and its values, is to first show several overpriced homes that really don't meet the prospect's needs. Finally, the agent shows a home that looks great by comparison and appears to be bargain-priced as well. The purpose of this practice is really deceit. What you believe to be a bargain might, in fact, be itself overpriced. Don't jump to make a purchase until you feel that you understand market values.

Value is subjective. What a realtor or a seller indicates is a special value to a home may be a feature you don't like or don't consider important. An agent may show you a home he or she considers "an exceptional value" at a price you consider excessive. Similarly, you might find homes that others feel are overpriced or fairly priced, but which you regard as bargains. People with good imaginations make excellent home finders. They often see what others fail to see. Sometimes a few dollars in interior and exterior decorating and minor remodeling will change the proverbial "sow's ear" into a "silk purse."

LIST PRICE VS. SALE PRICE

In a *seller's market*, in which there are few sellers and many buyers, actual sale prices are likely to be much closer to list prices than in a buyer's market. A *buyer's market* is one in which there are many sellers and fewer qualified buyers, and sale prices are likely to be considerably less than list prices. The buyer's market is a more prevalent market situation than a seller's market, and works to the benefit of buyers. Therefore, you would likely be within your financial purchasing ability by concentrating your home search on homes that list from 10 percent to 15 percent more than what you consider your maximum purchase price (based on your analysis in Chapter 3).

Generally, you will waste your time checking out homes priced significantly less than you are prepared to spend. If you are in the $100,000 housing range, you are not going to be happy with a home priced at $75,000, no matter how attractive the sales literature or how glib the agent.

However, as you will see in this chapter, there are "must sell" situations that offer you the opportunity to purchase not just at a fair market value but actually *below* market value.

When visiting new developments, keep in mind that, as a whole, large developers will not cut prices at all. Small builders with only a few homes for sale are usually more willing to negotiate.

When you are ready to visit homes, don't plan to spend too much time looking at those that are clearly beyond your financial capabilities. Doing so may make you unwilling to settle on a suitable home you *can* afford.

OPEN HOUSES

While you might buy a home as the result of visiting it as an *open house* (when a home that is for sale is open for viewing by the general public, without appointment), the primary advantage of open house visitations is that you're able to survey the market and get a basic feel for value without being under pressure or obligation. If you're observant and make careful comparisons, open houses can be a valuable house-hunting tool.

PICTURE BOOKLETS

In most areas of the country, private publishers and larger real estate firms produce free monthly or quarterly real estate guides. The guides include pictures—often in color—and glowing descriptions of properties that are represented by real estate firms. Some booklets are devoted entirely to new homes and subdivisions.

These guides are useful tools in helping you determine home values in given areas. Typically, homes that appear in such guides have curb appeal and are reasonably priced. You'll find these publications in racks in supermarkets and motels.

DEALING DIRECTLY WITH AN OWNER

Many home buyers avoid real estate agents. They want to deal directly with the existing owner, believing that because the seller is not paying a realtor's commission, the price of the home will be lower. True enough, most owners who deal without agents do so in order to avoid paying an agent's commission. But these owners also want to net more from the sale; they're not going to spend time and money in order to turn the savings over to a buyer. Studies of average home sale prices have shown that prices for homes sold directly by owners are not less than those for homes sold through agents.

Most people find it difficult to deal face to face with an owner. They either antagonize the owner by being critical of the home's features, or they fail to communicate with the owner because they don't want to be critical. The same people will take a completely different stance when dealing through an agent. They will raise every negative feature they can to validate a low offer.

Many owners who deal without agents are very sophisticated, and often look to take advantage of an unsophisticated buyer. They may want more than the property is worth, or they may want to sell without disclosing any problems. Before you sign a contract to buy from an owner, you should seek legal advice. A few dollars spent could prevent a disaster.

REAL ESTATE AGENTS

Real estate agents can help you. They can also save you a great deal of time and money.

Each real estate office controls a segment of the market through its listings. Through multiple listing services, they also have access to the majority of homes for sale in the areas you've pinpointed. If you were to limit yourself to "For Sale By Owner" properties, you would have access to only a small portion of the market.

You want an agent to spend his or her time and effort to find you a home. At the same time, to get this level of effort, you must let the agent know you are a serious buyer. A good approach is to ask friends and associates if they can recommend a real estate agent who deals in the geographical area or areas in which you are interested. Chances are, you will get several recommendations. When you contact an agent, mention the name of the person who made the recommendation. The agent will recognize that you are serious and that you would like to deal through that agent.

It's likely that you will find an agent early in your house-hunting who you feel is competent, whom you trust, and who you feel fully understands your situation and needs. Such an individual should be nurtured.

When dealing with an agent, you should carefully explain your needs. Be honest when discussing your financial limitations. Keeping information from the agent will only waste your time and the agent's.

When you see interesting classified ads from another broker, contact the agent with whom you are working. If an agent believes you are willing to work exclusively with him or her, that agent will become your eyes, ears, and legs, and will run down properties to meet your needs.

Always keep in mind that the agent represents the seller, not you, the buyer. The agent would prefer you buy one of his or her own listings so a sales commission can be earned. Next in preference would be that you buy one of the listings from the agent's office, which means a much higher commission than if you purchased another office's listing. Keep these agent priorities in mind. It is possible that they might even determine the agent's recommendations to you.

Because the agent represents the owner, he or she has a duty to keep the owner fully informed and to try to get as high an offer from you as possible. You should never tell the agent anything you would not want the owner to know.

Upon request, agents will provide you with actual sale price information about other homes. By knowing sale prices, you are preparing yourself to make an eventual offer on a home.

If an agent who understands your complete financial picture wants you to see a home priced beyond your means, it could be an indication that the price is negotiable. While a reputable seller's agent would not tell you this because of the agent's duty to the seller, the actions of the agent could betray the fact.

BUYER'S AGENTS

There are agents who, for a fee, will represent the buyer in a purchase. Such an agent would be an excellent investment for an unsophisticated buyer or in a situation where a home purchase must be made quickly. There are also agents who, while receiving part of the listing agent's commission, represent the buyer and elect not be sub-agents of the owner. Both types of buyer agents are still relatively rare, although many experts predict that buyer and seller representation will become normal procedure in the future.

CLASSIFIED ADS

Classified ads are the primary marketing tool for homes. You should regularly check the classifieds in all area newspapers. Because many owners tend to advertise in the papers they read, you will find ads, for example, in foreign-language papers that do not appear in the major dailies. You should also check weekly "throwaway" shoppers' papers. Because of their low ad costs, many owners use them.

Be aware that descriptions in classified ads tend to utilize superlatives that are often misleading. What an owner or broker describes as "luxurious" or "magnificent," you might regard with far less enthusiasm.

In addition to looking at ads that list homes for sale, check the ads that describe homes for rent. When an owner offers a home for rent with a lease option, it means that the owner would prefer to sell but can't afford to keep the property vacant for sale purposes. This could indicate a highly motivated seller which, in turn, could mean an excellent bargaining position for you.

When a rental home has a phone number or address outside of the immediate area, it could signal an excellent *purchase* opportunity. Such an owner would usually rather sell than rent, but renting is quicker. Investigate the owner's willingness to sell.

If an ad uses words such as "Asking $_____," "Submit all offers," "OBO" (or best offer), it means that the seller has already decided that a price cut is acceptable. You should consider investigating such homes, even if they are priced above what you feel you can afford.

When an ad indicates an owner "must sell," you are probably safe in assuming that the seller will accept considerably less than the asking price. Also, when the reason for the sale is included in the ad, the owner is generally seeking below-list price offers. Therefore, be alert for words such as "divorce," "transferred," "estate sale," "imminent foreclosure," "owner has two homes," etc. "Must sell" sellers increase the likelihood of a purchase at a realistic or even below-market price.

BULLETIN BOARDS

If you like an area, you should check bulletin boards in the area, such as those that appear in markets and laundromats. Often owners, especially elderly owners, will put a card on the board to save a few dollars rather than place an ad in the newspaper.

NETWORKING

When you are in the market for a home, let your friends, relatives, and business acquaintances know what you are looking for. By contacting a church of your denomination within the area you've selected, you can generally expect to get a great deal of help. A great many homes are sold that were never really on the market, simply because someone who was *considering* selling was told by a friend about someone who was looking to buy.

MOBILE HOMES

If you are searching for a used mobile home, you will likely find several real estate brokers who specialize in mobile home sales. Many mobile home dealers also handle the sale of units acquired in trade. On the other hand, because of the generally low resale value, many brokers either do not handle mobile home resales or, if they do, they are less than enthusiastic in their efforts. Due to this lack of enthusiasm, you will find a great percentage of "For Sale By Owner" units.

As you check the classified ads for mobile homes for sale, take a look at the mobile home rentals. Unless the unit is held for rent by an investor, the owner would likely be very receptive to a sale. In many communities, there are throwaway newspapers specifically aimed at mobile-home owners. These papers usually contain many "For Sale" ads.

A good place to look for mobile homes is the community bulletin boards at the mobile home parks you are interested in. Many mobile home equipment dealers also have bulletin boards and/or know of owners wishing to sell their units.

Another source is the park residents themselves. Not only are you likely to discover which homes are for sale, you'll learn which homes *will be* for sale in the future. In mobile home parks, residents are more likely to know what is happening in their park than are owners in coventional subdivisions. The reasons for this are the common-use facilities and park activities that bring the residents together.

At large parks that have security gates, ask the guard to direct you to the park manager. When you tell the manager that you are interested in locating within the park, you can expect the manager's cooperation.

BUYING BELOW MARKET

Every home seller hopes to get an above-market value price and every buyer hopes to purchase at a below-market value price. Because value is subjective, both buyer and seller often feel that they have been successful with the same sale.

There are special situations where a bargain price is likely. Generally, these situations involve highly motivated sellers who must sell now.

Foreclosures

If foreclosures interest you, check with the bank or savings and loan where you do your business and ask about homes they have in their inventory. Many lenders have a number of foreclosed properties and most are usually anxious to sell these properties.

Typically, they will sell the property for their financial interest in it, especially if it is a recent foreclosure, and they have done no work to make the property marketable.

An advantage of calling on an institution where you do business is that the lender will be more likely to carry the financing even with a comparatively low down payment. While some lenders will not cut the price they are asking, you should always request a 6 percent cut in price, since this is the typical commission the lender would pay if your offer were made through a broker. When a price cut is not possible, the same net effect can often be gained by an interest concession of one-half percent or more below-market rates and/or a lower loan origination fee.

Information on pending foreclosures is available at your county courthouse. This is a trip worth the effort since an owner facing imminent foreclosure is highly motivated; an attractive selling price could be your reward. However, while you can bid at foreclosure sales, such bids require that you be prepared to pay cash. Furthermore, the former owner might have a *redemption period*, during which he or she can regain control of the foreclosed property. It is strongly recommended that legal advice be obtained prior to a purchase in foreclosure or at the foreclosure sale. A purchaser could find that there are still priority *liens* or holds against the property and/or immediate possession is not possible.

Just because a property is a foreclosure doesn't mean it is a bargain. The reason many properties go to foreclosure is that more is owed against them than they are worth.

Auctions

Property is auctioned off for reasons other than foreclosure. There are voluntary auctions where the purpose is primarily to induce a quick sale. Developers are increasingly using this technique to close out developments; exceptional values are often possible.

Sometimes property auctions are court-mandated. These include sales by judgment creditors, property-tax sales, IRS auctions, and estate sales. In the case of creditor sales, there might be a redemption period of as long as one year (in addition, you may be getting only the seller's equity, not clear title). Check with an attorney before you look for this type of bargain.

At auction sales, you are generally required to hand over cash or a cashier's check for a percentage of the sale, often 10 percent. The balance must be presented within a prescribed period of time.

While auctions frequently result in bargain prices, they also can result in prices being paid that actually exceed the fair market value of the property. You must set your limits prior to an auction and not let your emotions take over. Often bidders feel hostile toward competing bidders and bid to win. Such a "win" is often an economic loss.

Evictions

By checking county records, you can obtain information on pending tenant evictions. Evictions from single-family housing may mean a frustrated owner who would love to sell. When people move up in housing, they sometimes decide to keep their old home for rental purposes. They like the idea of income. But in addition to income, they find that they also have headaches they did not contemplate, and they soon become fed up with the business of being landlords. If you find such an owner in the midst of eviction proceedings, you may discover exceptional purchase opportunities before the house is rerented. Frequently, evicted tenants leave homes in a mess. Being able to sell also allows the owner to escape the unpleasant job of clean-up and repair.

OVERPRICED CAN BE GOOD

Homes that are overpriced are usually overlooked by most would-be purchasers and real estate agents.

When listings of such homes expire, they are often relisted with other agents who have similar negative results. When an overpriced home has been on the market for an inordinate amount of time without any offers on it, an extremely attractive sales price is possible. Even if such a house, if priced properly, would still be slightly beyond your price range, it should be investigated. If you ask, agents will generally tell you about homes that have been for sale for one year or more. The owner of such a home could be ready for your below-market value offer.

FIXER-UPPERS

We tend to buy homes as much from emotion as from objective factors. The smell of fresh baked goods in an oven, bright flowers, sunshine streaming into a kitchen, fine furniture in a well-decorated room can all set the mood and prompt the urge to buy a particular property. Though it is difficult, do try to be objective. You should consider what a few dollars in decorations and landscaping can do.

Homes that are dirty, need repair, are poorly maintained, or just poorly decorated turn off many buyers. Most buyers are impressed with homes that show like models. They don't want to have to enter a new home with a shovel and scrub brush. But because many buyers are not interested in such properties, exceptional opportunities are possible.

If you can visualize what paint, decorating, and repairs can do, and can properly estimate labor and costs, you could end up with a true bargain. The owners of such property are generally highly motivated to sell. The result is that you as a buyer are in an exceptional bargaining position.

BARGAIN MANIA

Some would-be buyers look for impossible bargains. They pursue their dream of purchasing a

$150,000 home for $75,000. Some people actually house hunt for years. The result is that they hurt themselves. With real estate values in many areas of the country increasing at 10 percent or more per year, the cost of waiting for a bargain—even if it eventually materializes—could be much higher.

While price is always important, it should not be *the* most important factor in choosing a home. If you are not happy with the home, it is not a bargain, no matter what you paid for it.

LOOK IT OVER CAREFULLY

When you visit homes, be observant and look at the features that really matter. Don't let an owner's fine furniture influence your study of the structure, and know that paint and wallpaper are relatively inexpensive and can be changed at will. Don't let tasteful or tasteless decorating play a major part in your decision-making. What you want to observe are structural elements.

For example, the life-spans of roofs are directly related to the roof pitch. Steeper roofs last longer than roofs having a more gentle slope. You should look at the roof from the ground for visual problems, seeking evidence of repairs. Inside the home, check ceilings for leaks, especially in add-ons to the structure. For homes having flat roofs over fifteen years old, you should consider the probability that a reroofing will be required in the next few years. Homes having pitched roofs over 25 years old will require reroofing within a short period.

If there is central air-conditioning in addition to window air units, it could mean that the central unit is inadequate.

Cracks running diagonally from the corners of the foundation are generally caused by settling and usually are not a major concern. At the same time, they are good points to exploit during purchase negotiations.

Be alert for a basement waterline that indicates past flooding. If the basement walls have been painted, this fact could be hidden. It might be wise to check with neighbors and ask about water problems they may have experienced.

Be alert for any add-ons to the structure or conversions of nonliving space to living space. You want assurances that the work was done with a proper permit and is not a code violation. The local building department can give you this information. If the home contains space converted to a rental unit, you will also want to check the local zoning to see if the use is a violation.

Older homes often have boilers or furnaces that were once coal-fired but were converted to gas or oil. Generally, these furnaces are inefficient; replacement with a new unit may be necessary.

Be alert for pipes, boilers, furnaces, and air ducts in older homes that are wrapped with a white cloth or cement-like material. This is a probable sign of dangerous asbestos. Removal and disposal costs for asbestos can be considerable.

You should find out the type of insulation the home contains. A few years ago, formaldehyde foam insulation was used extensively. This type of insulation emits gases that can negatively affect health. And while the gases diminish with time, the presence of the insulation will negatively affect resale. The cost of removal is considerable. By removing an interior electrical wall-plate, you can determine the presence and type of insulation.

Insulation efficiency is expressed in "R" values. The higher the "R" rating, the better the insulation. Well-insulated homes have lower heating and cooling costs than homes that are less well-insulated. The amount of insulation may be especially important to you, particularly in cases of homes with flat roofs or cathedral ceilings where additional insulation cannot be easily added. Homes with 2-inch by 6-inch studs in their exterior walls (instead of the standard

2-inch by 4-inch studs) can be protected with greater insulation.

Remember that a home's windows are part of its insulation. Double panes of insulated glass or storm windows reduce heat loss, and triple panes are even better.

The home's electrical capacity is also important. Investigate the amp service to the home; as a bare minimum, you'll need 100-amp service. Also look for 220-volt wiring if you plan to run such large appliances as an electric stove or central air-conditioning.

CHECK WITH THE NEIGHBORS

When you are serious about purchasing a particular home, don't be shy about knocking on doors in the neighborhood. Tell the neighbors you are considering purchasing a home in the area, and ask if they can answer a few questions. People will generally welcome you into their homes and answer questions openly. Ask if they know of any particular problems with the house in which you are interested. Neighbors may remember repair trucks or recall owner complaints. If there were recent furnace repairs, for instance, and you discover the name of the firm, a call to the company could reveal that repairs were done when what was really needed was replacement.

The neighbors may know of recent home sales in the area and may have an idea of relative value. Their insights may support your feelings or may cause you to reevaluate your position. Neighbors may also know what the home's present owners paid for it— they may even know the down payment amount. This information is valuable for negotiating purposes.

Also of importance to you is the reason why the owner is selling. If the reason is job-related, the owner may be under pressure to sell the house quickly. Perhaps the owner is experiencing a money crunch or wishes to avoid sinking more money into home repairs. The seller's motivation will play a major part in your negotiation position.

DECISIONS, DECISIONS

When you are interested in several properties and undecided as to which is the best choice, revisit each of them and take notes. After doing so, ask yourself, "If the properties were priced identically, which one would I want?" Though the homes may be in the same general price range, you are setting aside the issue of price for a moment. Even if it means paying more, the home that pleases you more is the home you should purchase. A home that fails to give you a feeling of belonging and pride is not the home for you, regardless of its price. A home is a personal thing, and a few dollars' difference will be forgotten over the years you live in and enjoy your home.

AVOID CONFUSION

When visiting a great many homes over a period of weeks or even months, it is easy to become confused, attributing features of one home to another. When looking at homes with an agent, ask for photocopies of the multiple listing sheets on the homes you are to visit. Customarily, these sheets include a photograph of the house. The sheets also list features and include comments, though it's wise to add your own on the back. As an alternative, you can take photographs of homes you find interesting and note the address and any comments you have on the back of the photo. By using either of these methods, you can avoid confusion and will be better prepared to select for second viewings.

Chapter 6:
Negotiations and Buying Strategies

One of the most important aspects of buying a home is the negotiation process between buyer and seller. Knowing where you stand and understanding the options and strategies you can employ are vital if you are to be successful in negotiating the kind of home purchase you want.

THE SELLER'S AGENT

When dealing with a real estate agent, keep in mind that the agent represents the seller and has a fiduciary duty to him or her. This is a position of financial and legal trust. To help *you* buy the home at the lowest possible price would be a violation of that trust. Actually, the agent really has a duty to get you, the buyer, to pay as much as possible for the property. Also, remember that the agent's commission is customarily a percentage of the sale price, so the higher the price, the higher the commission earned.

DON'T SHOW YOUR DESIRE

Try not to let an agent know how much you really want the house you are bidding on if you are offering less than market value. If the agent knows you are in love with the house, he or she will likely recommend that the owner either counter your offer or hold firm on price.

In the same manner, never indicate to an agent that you will pay more than you are offering. If you do, you might as well increase your offer right away.

THE TWO-HOUSE STRATEGY

Chances are, you'll find several homes that interest you. If Home #1 has features or a price that appeals to you, it's perfectly legitimate to express your thoughts about that home to the agent who represents Home #2. If Home #1 is available at a lower price than Home #2, let the agent know you're willing to make an offer on Home #2 at that lower price. It's likely that the agent, who doesn't want to lose a commission, will relay your thoughts to the owners he is representing. By using this "second-house" strategy, you effectively have the seller's agent working for you to gain an acceptance of your offer for Home #2.

MOTIVATION

The more motivated the seller, the tougher you can be in negotiations. This means you can start out with a relatively low offer and have a reasonable hope of acceptance. If the owner gives you a counteroffer, you should consider countering it, rather than accepting it outright. If the seller is highly motivated, your second offer has a good chance of being accepted.

WHAT THE OWNER PAID

As discussed in Chapter 5, any information you have on what the owner paid for the property can be valuable in determining what to offer. If the neighbors can't give you a specific figure, ask how long the owners have lived in the home. Knowing when owners purchased should give you a general idea of what they paid. Or, if there is an FHA or VA loan on the property, knowing the balance and how long the owners have owned will give you a good idea about the purchase price, since the purchase was likely made with a minimum down payment or none at all. By checking county records, you can find the *reve-*

nue stamps on the seller's deed. The clerk in your county recorder's office will explain how to compute purchase price based on these stamps.

It is an advantage to know what a seller paid, because sellers who have experienced a significant increase in value are much more likely to accept an offer that is less than list price and/or market value. For example, assume an owner paid $30,000 for a home fifteen years ago. Assume also that the owner is asking $110,000 for the property. If you offered $90,000, the offer might be viewed favorably by the owner. The reduction from the list price is not cost but profit. The owner is still making a $60,000 profit, or 200 percent, on the purchase price.

If, however, in the case above the owner had paid $95,000, then your offer would result in a loss. Very likely your $90,000 offer would not be accepted and might even antagonize the owner.

NEW ON THE MARKET

Assume a property has just been put on the market and you want to buy it. Even if you are willing to pay full price, do not make an offer that fully meets the seller's price and terms. Doing so will convince the owners that they underpriced their home and are giving it away. Thus, though the owners may accept your full offer, they might look for ways to get out of their agreement.

A better approach is to offer several thousand dollars less than the asking price and slightly alter some of the terms or provisions of the contract. Allow twenty-four hours or less for acceptance. Even if the owners refuse your offer, a later full-price offer will make the owners feel they got what they wanted by their tough negotiation.

FULL-PRICE OFFER

There are times when it is appropriate to make full-price offers. In a seller's market or when you are aware of another party's interest, and you are sure this is the house for you, offer full price. A full-price offer is also appropriate when you are certain that the house, as offered, is a terrific bargain.

EXPLAIN YOUR POSITION

When making an offer below list price, you don't want to appear arbitrary. Explain to the seller's agent or to the owner how you arrived at the price. It could be the price of another equally desirable property. It could be because the home requires repairs. Or, simply enough, it could be the maximum amount you can finance on your income. If you appear arbitrary, the seller is likely to resent you and take a tougher bargaining stance. Your goal is to make the owner *want* to sell to you.

COMPETING OFFERS

After you submit an offer, the owners (assuming no agent is involved) might indicate that there is another offer in as well, and that you are expected to bid against the other would-be buyer. You don't want to be in an auction situation. It could likely end up with your overpaying a significant amount to buy the house.

The competing offer could be a nonexistent negotiation ploy, a nonbinding verbal offer, or a very real written offer. Not knowing the true nature of the offer, take the initiative and ask to see it. If such an offer exists at a price higher than yours, and if you still are interested, counter with: *"If you wish, I will give you a written offer with two minutes to accept it or reject it. No further offers will be made by me. If this is not satisfactory with you, then I wish to revoke my offer and want all copies returned to me."*

What you are doing is indicating that you will not play a bidding game. If the sellers return your offer, they lose their leverage against the other offerer. You have already indicated that you would beat the earlier offer. In all likelihood, this tactic will induce the owner to see your new offer. Your new offer should be at least several thousand dollars higher than the competing offer.

If an agent is involved, you can agree to work with the agent, but insist that the owners be present. You cannot allow the agent the opportunity to solicit the other buyer to beat your offer. The owners and agent must feel that your position is firm, and that your offer is a now or never proposition.

DON'T BE RIGID

Don't allow yourself to lose a house you really want because of an insignificant dollar amount. As an example, assume an owner wants $110,000 for a home and you offer $100,000. Assume also that the owner counters with $102,000. If you now take the position that you won't pay a dime more than $100,000, you could lose the house for what amounts to a two-percent difference. Standing firm can show character, but it could leave you with a decision you could regret for years. In terms of a $100,000 purchase, $2,000 is not really significant. Financing an additional $2,000 over 25 years at 10 percent interest means a payment increase of only $18.18 a month.

URGENCY

Be cautious if an agent or owner indicates an extreme sense of urgency. While there could be another person interested in the home, it's more likely you're experiencing a seller's ploy. Far better to lose a house to another buyer than to buy before you are certain the property is the one you really want.

On the other hand, while agents and owners are customarily the ones who try to stampede a buyer into purchasing, the situation can be easily reversed. Don't give sellers long to accept your offer. If the owners are in the same geographical area, consider giving 24 hours for acceptance. This puts the urgency on the seller and also reinforces your position that you are interested in other property(ies).

Granting too much time for acceptance will also give an owner a chance to discuss your offer with friends and relatives. Unfortunately, the frequent advice is, "Your home is worth more than that." This advice is easy to give, even though it might not be in the owner's best interests.

"AS IS"

Avoid buying a property "as is" even when suggested by an agent. Be especially concerned when an owner suggests an "as is" sale. If "as is" is used at all, it should be for a particular item or system and you should fully understand the condition of that item or system.

In some states, courts have held that "as is" does not protect sellers when they failed to inform buyers about a hidden defect or concealed the problem.

CONDITION GUARANTEE

Your offer should normally be contingent upon all electrical, mechanical, and plumbing equipment and systems being in good and proper working order at the time of the sale. Depending upon the location of the home, you might also want to ascertain that there is no insect infestation or structural damage. Clauses such as the following should be included:

"Sellers agree that within (number of) days prior to closing, buyers and/or buyers' representatives shall be allowed to inspect the property to verify that all electrical, mechanical, and plumbing equipment and systems are in good and proper working order. Sellers agree to disclose in writing to buyers by (date) any defects in the property known by him or her. Sellers agree to rectify defects so disclosed or discovered by buyers at sellers' expense prior to close of sale.

"Within _____ calendar days of sellers' acceptance, sellers shall furnish buyers at sellers' expense a current report by a licensed structural pest control operator that there is no infestation of wood-destroying pests. Any work recommended to correct damage caused by infestation shall be performed at sellers' expense."

CONTINGENCIES

The more contingencies included in an offer, the less the likelihood of acceptance. Sellers want certainties. Nevertheless, there are instances when contingencies should be used.

Financing Contingency

If your offer requires new financing and you are unsure of your ability to obtain the required financing, or you wish to be protected against having to complete the sale should interest rates rise dramatically, consider the advantages of a financing contingency. An example of a financing contingency clause is as follows:

"This offer is contingent upon the buyer obtaining a new loan in the amount of $_____, payable monthly at no more than $_____ with interest rate not to exceed _____%. Fixed rate and loan origination costs are not to exceed $_____."

Contingent Upon Approval

One way to tie up a property for several days without being bound to complete the purchase is with an offer contingent upon the approval of another person, such as a spouse. This contingency is common when one spouse is not yet in the area. However, such a provision should require approval within a reasonable period of time, such as one week, or it will likely be rejected.

Appraisal Contingency

If you have found a home you want but are unsure of its value, consider an offer contingent upon an appraisal of no less than the purchase price. An example of such a clause would be:

"This offer is contingent upon purchaser obtaining an appraisal, at purchaser's expense, by (date) from an authorized appraiser chosen by purchaser indicating a value of not less than the purchase price."

OPTIONS TO PURCHASE

An excellent way to hold available property is by using an *option to purchase*. Option forms are available at most large stationery stores. With an option, you have a contract that gives you the right to form a contract. You have the right to purchase property at an agreed price and terms, if you wish to do so, within a stated period of time.

To be binding, consideration must be given to the owner in exchange for the option. An excellent option method is to give a rather small amount of money for a short-term option, but to provide for an extension by paying an additional, much larger fee. In the buyer's best interest, the option should provide that the option fee shall apply toward the purchase price of the home.

If you do not have a necessary down payment and a seller is unwilling to provide seller-financing, the seller might be receptive to a *lease option* whereby you become a tenant with the right to purchase. Owners feel that tenants under option agreements are more likely than ordinary renters to maintain a property. With a lease option, separate monetary consideration for the option need not be given; the rent would serve this purpose. As a potential buyer holding an option, you would want as much of the rent as possible to apply toward the purchase price. By renting, you would be accumulating your down payment.

EARNEST MONEY DEPOSIT

Earnest money is the buyer's deposit that accompanies an offer to purchase. Earnest money indicates to the seller that the buyer is serious. If the offer is refused by the seller, the earnest money is returned to the buyer. Should the buyer default after an offer is accepted, the agreement normally would provide for the forfeiture of the earnest money deposit. Some buyers try to tie up property with small earnest money deposits. The net effect is that they have purchased an option to buy by using their deposit as the option price. Because of this tactic, many sellers demand substantial earnest money deposits.

Understandably, owners are impressed by large deposits; a large deposit makes it more difficult for an owner to turn down an offer. Consider giving the largest deposit possible with your offer. If an agent is involved, the deposit check should be made out to the agent's trust account or to a neutral third party that will hold the money until the transaction is complete; this third party is known as an *escrow company*. Be sure to instruct the agent that the check is not to be deposited until the offer is accepted. In this way, you will not have to withdraw money from savings to cover the check until the offer is accepted.

When dealing directly with an owner, do not allow the owner to have access to your deposit. You could find yourself in a situation where the owner has spent the money and then is unable to deliver marketable title to the property. One option is to make the deposit check out to your attorney's trust account. Or, the check could be made out to an independent escrow firm or bank escrow account. In any event, the check should indicate its purpose and should be attached to the face of the offer.

VERBAL UNDERSTANDINGS

As any attorney will tell you, never rely on verbal agreements. All aspects of your negotiations—no matter how minor—should be set forth firmly in writing, and become part and parcel of the formal purchase agreement. This advice is backed by law: Under the *Parol Evidence Rule*, all verbal agreements are assumed to be merged in the formal contract when it is written; any parol, or extrinsic, evidence or claims not cited in the contract will not be allowed to vary the terms of the contract. For example, the seller tells you he will leave five cords of firewood, but upon closing, you discover the wood is gone. The seller may not have been intentionally dishonest, but unless this provision was written in the purchase agreement, you would have little recourse if later you tried to claim the wood. Make certain all provisions are included as part of your written purchase agreement.

ATTORNEYS

It's unfortunate but true: As a buyer, you generally have no protection from your own mistakes. If you sign a contract that you failed to read or did not fully understand, you could be bound to its terms. Although state laws provide protection against fraud and unscrupulous dealings, the proverb, "an ounce of prevention is worth a pound of cure," is applicable to real estate purchases. If you don't fully understand an agreement, or any portion of it, or if the purchase agreement was drawn by the sellers, legal advice should be sought. Don't rely exclusively on the advice of your real estate agent, particularly on such matters as taking possession of a property, or the tax ramifications of ownership. Your best bet is to find an attorney with specialized real estate knowledge. Most larger law firms are staffed with this expertise. If you need assistance finding appropriate legal advice, contact your local bar association.

Know that when you work with an attorney, however, you are working with a person who has been trained in the law, but who may not be experienced in finance or business decision-making. Many attorneys provide advice that extends beyond the limits of their expertise, and that may be given without a full understanding of your wants and needs or the owner's position. The net effect of following such nonlegal advice could be a failed sale. Follow the advice your attorney is qualified to give; if you'll be most comfortable with an attorney who specializes in real estate law, get one.

PRESENTING OFFER TO OWNER

If an agent is not involved in the purchase negotiations, you will be presenting your offer directly to the owners. Before you do so, deliberate carefully what you will offer and what concessions, if any, you will be willing to make. Remember that the owner has likely asked for more than he or she hopes to get.

Some people prepare their offer forms before they arrive at the owners' home. A better technique is to know what you will include and write the offer in front of the owners. Keep in mind that you want the offer to be simple, with as few contingencies as possible to increase the likelihood of its acceptance. You don't want to confuse the owners.

Don't present an offer when the seller's children, relatives, or friends are present. You don't want any interruptions, nor do you want to end up negotiating with a whole group of people. Chances are, friends and relatives will be supportive of the owner and give "hang tough" advice, even though it may not be in the owners' best interests.

You should suggest that you all sit at the kitchen table. You want both spouses present if the sellers are a married couple. If you are married, your spouse should be with you. The kitchen table provides close physical contact and a nonhostile environment. It is more difficult for a seller to take a strong defensive position in such an environment.

NEGOTIATION TACTICS

Begin your negotiations on a positive, friendly note. Compliment the owners about some aspect of their home that you like, such as the garden or the decor. Then tell the owners a little about yourself; you want them to like you. Next, discuss the house and what you liked about it. Also tell them about an alternative home you like and why you like it, though emphasizing that you decided to work out a purchase of *their* home, if possible.

If you prepared a completed offer in advance, do not simply hand it over; the first thing the owners will do is look for the price. Instead, discuss other points of the offer. If you are filling in the form in front of the owners, do so as each point is agreed to. For example, you want to agree on date or dates of closing and possession, and what is or isn't to be included with the sale. To be reasonable, you can give in on minor points. Be sure to cover all points on the offer form.

The *last* item to cover is price and owner financing, if any. Before you write in or state the price, give a little background on how you arrived at the price, and the criteria you used. You don't want the owners to feel you are being arbitrary or are trying to take advantage of them. You want to appear forthright and reasonable. Then, write down the price, sign the offer, and hand it to your spouse for his or her signature. Extend the offer forms and a check to the owners. Leave a pen on the table.

A Truce
If you run into strong resistance, a good ploy is to call a temporary truce. You can do this by asking for a cup of coffee. The break will tend to relieve the tension. Spend the time asking questions about the neighbors. A short break can do wonders toward arriving at a reasonable solution to an impasse.

Quote Other Prices

To convince the owner that your offer is fair and reasonable, produce advertisements of other homes or properties in the area that are listed in the price range you are willing to pay for this particular home. Similarly, knowing actual sale prices will help you.

If the owners bring up what others in the neighborhood are asking for their homes, respond by asking how long these homes have been on the market. You can then point out that they have not been sold. Be sure to explain that asking prices are meaningless as points of comparison; it is actual *sale* prices that are important.

If an owner cites someone who received a particular price, counter by asking what the sale terms were. The owner probably would not know. Explain how lower interest could mean a higher price (if you are offering cash). Also, point out that sellers tend to inflate what they sold their homes for because it makes them appear to be clever business people.

In your price negotiations, you should also emphasize any work the home may require and its probable cost. The owners will be well aware of any deficiencies the house has.

"Let's Split the Difference"

When an owner counters your offer to purchase with a higher price, an excellent technique is to say, *"Let's split the difference."* In other words, what you're offering to do is to split between the original offer and the counteroffer, not the asking price. Though there is no logical basis that makes splitting the difference a fair solution, people believe that it's a fair compromise.

DON'T POSTPONE ACCEPTANCE

Generally, it is best not to allow postponement of an acceptance decision. The result will usually be a rejection. Try to work out problems together when the offer is presented. Also, you don't want to give the owners the opportunity to talk to other people who are not qualified to advise them.

THE ACCEPTANCE

In the case of jointly owned property, you want the acceptance signed by both owners. A legal remedy available to buyers when the sellers default is *specific performance*. Under this remedy, the buyers legally force the sellers to honor their agreement and convey the property. This remedy is not available if all owners have not agreed to the sale.

COUNTEROFFER

When an owner gives a counteroffer, he or she is really saying, "No I won't accept your offer, but I will accept (dollar amount)." By signing the counteroffer, you, as buyer, can form a binding contract. An alternative would be to counter the counteroffer. Your countering is a rejection and you are precluded from later acceptance; once countered, an offer is dead. Your counter to the counteroffer is, therefore, really a new original offer.

BUYER'S REMORSE

Once you make an offer to purchase a home you will likely suffer what is known as buyer's remorse. You will wonder if you did the right thing. This feeling of uncertainty is common; most buyers have known it. Often it is accelerated by "friends" who tell you that you paid too much or indicate you should have purchased somewhere else. The result for some buyers is that they get cold feet and revoke their offer.

By understanding that your feelings of doubt are normal, you will be less likely to panic and withdraw from purchasing a home that you truly wanted.

Chapter 7:
Financing and Mortgages

Unless you are one of the few who will pay for your home with cash, you will probably adopt a financing arrangement. The purpose of this chapter is to discuss the various aspects and ramifications of financing and mortgage loans.

Once you have determined the monthly payment amount you can afford to make for a home, you can easily determine by the use of amortization tables the amount you can finance based on prevailing interest rates; sample tables are in Chapter 3. If lower interest rate loans can be assumed, or if sellers will carry financing at below-market interest rates, the amount you can finance with the same payment will increase.

EARLY LOAN CONSIDERATION

You should contact your local bank and savings and loan institutions early in your house-hunting process in order to find out about available financing. There are also mortgage companies that make a wide variety of loans that they then sell to other lenders. Mortgage companies will often handle FHA and VA loans which offer some advantages; however, many lenders avoid these types of loans because of the extensive paperwork involved. Your state might also offer loans for particular groups of people, such as veterans. For small towns and rural areas, you might want to investigate the Federal Farm Home Loan office; they offer a variety of loan programs. In any event, understanding the types and terms of available new financing will help you in your house-hunting efforts.

YOUR CREDIT RATING

Your credit rating is extremely important in obtaining a new loan. It is even important in seller financing. While a few sellers will handle financing without a credit report, sophisticated sellers will want to know about your credit. When an agent is involved, he or she will likely recommend a credit check if the seller is going to be financing the purchaser.

Some people have always paid cash and thus have no credit history. Unfortunately, these people would have great difficulty obtaining a home loan. Lenders are leery of buyers who have no history of meeting their obligations. They also sometimes feel that there is something wrong with a person who has no credit history.

Ways to establish credit include applying for gasoline credit cards and credit cards from local stores. These are usually easier to get than major credit cards. You should charge purchases on the new cards and pay them off immediately when billed. Using these cards as a credit record, you can then apply for a major national credit card through your bank. Use the same charge and pay procedures. You should consider obtaining several major credit cards.

Computerized credit data is kept on everyone who has established and used credit. Under the Federal Fair Credit Reporting Act, you have the right to know the substance of the material in your credit file. If an adverse action is taken against you because of your credit rating, you have the right to know the reasons. You also have the right to have disputed material investigated, and you can place a statement of explanation of any dispute in your file.

PRIMARY AND SECONDARY FINANCING

Primary financing refers to *first mortgages;* secondary financing refers to *second mortgages*. The distinction is one of priority: The first loan that is recorded is the first mortgage; mortgages recorded after the first mortgage are considered junior to the first and are second mortgages. In case of a foreclosure sale, the mortgages are paid off in the order of their priority. Second mortgages carry more risk than first mortgages because of the possibility that foreclosure sale proceeds would be not be sufficient to pay them off.

MORTGAGES

In most states, *mortgages* are the preferred financing instrument. The *mortgagor* is the buyer (or borrower) who gives to the *mortgagee* (lender) a lien or title transfer (the mortgage) to secure a loan or payment for the property. The mortgagor gives the mortgagee a promissory note for the amount being financed. As security for the note, the mortgagor gives the mortgagee a mortgage.

```
Mortgagor ————— Mortgage ————→Mortgagee
(Borrower) ————— Note —————→(Lender)
```

Should a mortgagor default on note payments, the mortgagee would foreclose on the mortgage. In some states, the mortgagor has a long period to redeem the property after foreclosure; in other states, redemption rights are limited.

TRUST DEEDS

In some parts of the country, *trust deeds* are the preferred financing instruments. A trust deed is a three-party transaction where the *truster* (borrower) gives a note to the *beneficiary* (the lender or, if financing the buyer, the seller). As security for the note, the truster gives legal title to a third party known as the *trustee*. Should the truster default, the trustee conducts a foreclosure sale that ends the purchaser's interests, usually with no right of redemption after the sale. Features of trust deeds over mortgages, in those states where they are used, are a shorter foreclosure time and no truster redemption rights.

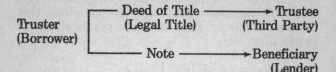

Truster (Borrower)	— Deed of Title (Legal Title) ——→ Trustee (Third Party)
	— Note ——————→ Beneficiary (Lender)

LAND CONTRACTS

Under a *land contract*, the seller finances the purchaser. The seller keeps title to the property and the buyer gets possession. The buyer does not generally receive a deed until the buyer has paid off the contract. An advantage of such a sale to sellers is that, in many states, the seller can obtain a quick and inexpensive foreclosure or forfeiture of the buyer's right to purchase should the buyer default. Because of the ease of foreclosure, sellers are often willing to negotiate a sale with a comparatively small down payment.

For buyers, land contracts can be dangerous in that the seller might be unable to deliver a clear title when the contract is paid off. In some states, this can be overcome with title insurance for the land contract purchaser. At the very least, a purchaser would want a preliminary title check to ascertain that the seller has a marketable title. Additionally, he or she needs a recording of the contract. By recording, the purchaser would have priority over most subsequent lienholders. Because land contract purchaser rights vary considerably from state to state, it is strongly recommended that legal advice be sought prior to purchasing a home on a land contract.

DEFICIENCY JUDGMENTS

In the event a foreclosure sale brings less than is due on the foreclosing mortgage, a *deficiency judgment* might be possible. This is a court determination that the foreclosed former homeowner is still indebted to the lender for the deficiency.

In some states, deficiency judgments are not allowed. In other states, they are limited to specific loan situations. Don't buy a home thinking you can just walk away from it if you want out. Your obligations will depend on the laws of the state in which you live.

TYPES OF MORTGAGE LOANS

Straight Mortgages
Straight mortgages are interest-only loans. The entire loan principal then outstanding must be repaid when due. While the idea of having to pay only the interest is intriguing, it is not a good idea if you can pay the few dollars more it takes to amortize the loan. For example, a monthly interest-only payment on a $50,000 straight loan at 10 percent would be $416.67. To amortize the loan over 30 years would require a payment of $439.00, or only $22.33 more per month.

Amortized Mortgages
Amortized mortgages are loans that are paid off fully with equal monthly installments. The longer the amortization period, the lower the monthly payment.

Rollover Loans
Many lenders whose portfolios included long-term mortgages were hurt when interest rates rose. In many cases, their average cost of borrowing money exceeded their average return on their mortgages, re-

sulting in huge losses. Lenders do not want to be faced by a situation such as this again. A solution has been shorter-term loans.

The *rollover* is a short-term loan, usually five years. Payments, however, are based on a 20- or 25-year amortization period. After five years, the buyer has the option of either paying the loan off in full, or having the lender write a new loan for five years at the then prevailing interest rate. A problem for borrowers is that these rollover loans do not generally have a cap on interest rates. A borrower could be in serious trouble should there be a significant increase in interest rates after five years.

10- to 15-Year Loans

Lenders have been receiving excellent consumer response to short-term, fixed-rate amortized 10- and 15-year loans. The shorter term reduces the lender's risk of being locked into long-term loans at rates below their cost of funds. In addition, the shorter amortization quickly increases the equity of the borrower, reducing the likelihood of default. Because of these lender advantages, 10- and 15-year loans often have lower initial loan costs and/or carry a lower interest rate than longer-term, fixed-rate home loans. A one-half percent lower rate for a 15-year loan compared with a 30-year loan is fairly common.

Payments on a 15-year amortized loan are about 20 percent greater than on a 30-year amortized loan having the same interest rate. If, as a borrower, you can afford the higher payments, the short-term loan offers significant economic advantages. The increased payment would reduce the total interest you must pay by more than 50 percent. For example, suppose you have a 30-year amortized loan for $100,000 at 11 percent with payments of $953.00 per month. You will have paid $242,838 in interest over the life of the loan. However, a payment of only $184.00 more per month would amortize the $100,000 over 15 years. A payment of $424.51 more would amortize the $100,000 over 10 years. The accompanying table illustrates the interest savings available with shorter-term loans.

MONTHLY PAYMENTS ON A $100,000 LOAN (11% INTEREST) FOR VARIOUS LOAN PERIODS

Loan Period	Monthly Payment	Total Interest Paid
30 years	$ 953.00	$242,838
15 years	$1137.00	$104,588
10 years	$1377.51	$ 65,301

Besides the huge savings in interest with a short-term loan, the homeowner is more likely to have a home free and clear of encumbrances at the time of retirement. Too, the fast equity buildup provides a savings source that can be drawn upon for emergencies or children's education.

Critics of short-term amortized loans point out that the borrower would be ahead if he or she invested the difference in payments at a rate higher than that they are paying on the 30-year loan. However, as a practical matter, the likelihood of a homeowner regularly saving this amount each month is remote. In addition, safe investments at a rate above a standard mortgage rate are not readily available. If they were, lenders would make them and forget about home loans.

Biweekly Mortgages

Mortgages with biweekly payments (every other week) were first used in Canada and have been gaining popularity in the United States. Under these loans, the borrower makes a payment every two weeks equal to half the monthly mortgage amount. There are several consumer advantages to such loans.

To begin with, people are generally paid on a weekly or biweekly basis. Because monthly payments do not relate to paychecks, budgeting may be difficult for many people. The biweekly payment can be arranged to fall on a payday, allowing for much easier consumer budgeting. An even greater advantage is that the buyer is making 26 payments per year, or the equivalent of 13 monthly payments per year. The result is that a 30-year amortized loan is actually paid up in about 18 years.

Lenders like biweekly payments since they shorten the payment period. They do not, however, like the paperwork of additional payments. To cut costs, some lenders provide for automatic withdrawal from borrowers' accounts. In addition to biweekly loans, some Canadian lenders have weekly payment plans. We can expect to see such loans in the future in the United States.

Fixed- and Adjustable-Rate Loans

The interest rate on a *fixed-rate loan* remains the same over the life of the loan. The borrower knows at the outset what his or her monthly payments will be, and that the payments will always be the same. In contrast, *adjustable-rate loans* are loans in which the interest rate can change, based on some specified criterion, such as the interest rate on Treasury bills or the average national mortgage rate. Because interest rates can increase, the dollar amount of the mortgage payments can increase as well; many people have ended up in foreclosure when their adjustable-rate loan payments rose beyond their ability to pay.

Under a new rule promulgated by the Federal Reserve Board, creditors are required to distribute to consumers an educational booklet about adjustable-rate mortgage loans, and to provide a detailed description of the variable rate feature. Consumers are to receive this information upon receipt of a loan application form or before paying a nonrefundable fee, whichever is earlier. Because the rule creates a standard set of disclosures for adjustable-rate loans, creditors are relieved of the burden of compliance with different disclosure requirements imposed by the various federal financial regulatory agencies. This ruling went into effect December 28, 1987, but creditor compliance is optional until October 1, 1988.

Lenders frequently offer a very low, short-term "teaser" rate to encourage the use of these loans. If you use an adjustable rate loan, make certain there is a maximum interest cap. Generally, these caps are 5 to 6 percent over the loan's initial rate. With a 5 percent cap, a 9 percent initial rate could never exceed 14 percent interest. Additionally, there are normally caps on the number of times the rate can be increased each year. Typically, there can be no more than one or two interest changes per year, and the total annual increase cannot exceed 2 percent.

If you intend to refinance or sell a home within a few years, a lower adjustable-rate loan might offer significant interest savings over a higher fixed-rate loan.

In addition to the value of the property, lenders consider the income of the borrower when determining the amount they will allow the borrower to finance. Because adjustable-rate loans have lower base interest rates, a borrower can qualify for a larger adjustable-rate loan based on his or her income than would otherwise be possible using a fixed-rate loan. Therefore, if you need a larger loan than is available at a fixed rate, an adjustable-rate should be considered.

If the interest for fixed-rate loans should fall below an adjustable-rate loan, you would probably want to refinance, and lock in the lower rate. Some adjustable-rate loans provide for conversion to fixed rates without penalty; however, most require a conversion charge.

Graduated-Payment Mortgages

There are a number of mortgages geared for younger professionals whose incomes can be expected to increase in the near future. These loans are generally known as *graduated-payment mortgages* (GPMs). Under these mortgages, the borrower's payments for the first few years are very low; thereafter, they increase annually. These loans help young buyers become homeowners with current payments based on current income and future payments increasing as income is expected to increase. Because of the escalating payments, these loans result in an amortization over a short period, such as 15 years.

Lenders usually demand large down payments on these loans since, during the first few years, there is negative amortization. In other words, the payments are not sufficient to cover the interest, causing the amount owed actually to increase.

Sharing Appreciation Mortgages

A number of television seminar presenters have espoused *sharing appreciation mortgages* (SAMs). The objective is to buy with a low or no down payment and offer to sell the same way. There is an agreement between the buyer and the seller to place the home on the market within a stated period of time, such as five years, with the sale profits to be split between the two parties. This kind of arrangement would be advantageous for sellers if they could find buyers willing to give up half the appreciation on their homes. However, because of the difficulty of finding such buyers, few ever succeed in structuring such a sale. As a purchaser, you deserve the appreciation on a home after paying the principal and interest. Be wary of these shared appreciation mortgages.

FHA Loans

Federal Housing Administration (FHA) loans are low down payment housing loans. The FHA, as a branch of the federal government, insures loans made by approved lending institutions, thus protecting the lender against the risk of default. To obtain this type of loan, an FHA appraisal is required, and the property must meet minimum requirements. Because the loan cannot exceed the appraisal, the borrower obtains some protection as to the home's value.

You, as borrower, pay for this insurance at the time of the loan. The cost of the insurance is added to the loan amount. On the other hand, FHA loan interest is often less than conventional interest because the lender is protected by the insurance. Maximum loan amounts are set by the FHA, but the maximum varies in different areas. FHA loans are generally assumable by anyone, and there are no prepayment penalties.

Unfortunately, time delays are common in processing FHA loans; generally, they take considerably longer than conventional loans. Furthermore, not every lender in your area will process FHA loans. If your bank or savings and loan does not handle them, they can direct you to a lender who does.

VA Loans

Qualified veterans can obtain VA loans for housing. VA loans are guaranteed by the federal government. If you feel you are eligible for a VA loan, you can submit a copy of your discharge and obtain a certificate of eligibility. VA loans require no down payment, although lenders may require one. VA loans are fully assumable and may be assumed by a nonveteran.

FINANCING YOUR LOAN

The ins and outs of financing mortgage loans—the requisites and the options—can be confusing, especially to the uninitiated. Loan officers and agents can advise you; however, the better you understand financing, the more assured you'll be when arranging a loan and assuming its obligations.

Private Mortgage Insurance

Many conventional lenders insist on *private mortgage insurance* (PMI) in order to protect themselves against default on the loan, particularly if your down payment is less than 20 percent of the purchase price. An amount is generally added to each of your monthly mortgage payments to cover this insurance. You are thus paying to insure your lender against your own default. Once your equity increases to 20 percent of the purchase price from amortization of the mortgage loan, payments for PMI should cease.

Loan Points and Costs

As a fee to make the loan, most lenders demand several *loan points*. Each point is one percent of the loan amount. A lender requiring three points on a $100,000 loan is asking for $3,000 as a fee to make the loan. Also known as the *loan origination fee*, points are frequently added to the loan; in the case above, the note would total $103,000 although the lender paid out only $100,000. Lenders justify points by claiming they are necessary to make the loan competitive. In other words, the absence of points would simply mean higher interest rates. In addition to points, some lenders may charge additional fees, such as three points plus $300.

The Consumer Protection Act of 1968, also known as the Truth-in-Lending Act, requires lenders to state interest as an *annual percentage rate* (APR). This rate takes into account the loan origination fees so that the APR would be higher than the interest rate set forth on the note. When comparing rates among various lenders, use the APR as your measure.

There are also loan costs, such as appraisal fees and credit report fees. These fees vary among lenders and should also be considered and compared when making financing decisions.

If you anticipate paying off a loan in a fairly short time, such as one or two years, you would probably be better off with a loan having lower loan costs but a higher rate of interest. On the other hand, if you expect to remain in a home for 20 years, you would want a loan having a lower interest rate, even though the initial loan costs are higher.

Down Payments

Because of high foreclosure rates in many parts of the country during the early 1980s, many lenders have increased their down payment requirements.

The rate of foreclosure is directly related to the size of down payments. A property purchased with a no or low down payment is much more likely to end up in a foreclosure situation than a home purchased with a substantial down payment. This is true largely because a buyer who has put down a large down payment has more to lose than an investor who put down little or no money. In other words, the buyer who has put down a substantial down payment has more incentive to meet his mortgage obligations.

LOAN ASSUMABILITY

If a loan document says nothing about *assumability* (a buyer's option to take on responsibility for the liability of a present loan-holder), the loan can be assumed.

VA loans and FHA loans made prior to 1987 are assumable by any purchaser. However, loans that state they are not assumable, or are due in full upon sale, may not be assumed.

Due-On-Sale Clauses

A *due-on-sale clause* prohibits the assumption of a loan and is fully enforceable. Most loans made by institutional lenders, such as banks, savings and loans, and insurance companies, include due-on-sale clauses, as do loans by many private lenders.

These clauses give the lenders a chance to reevaluate the interest rate. If the interest rate has remained the same or fallen since the time of the original loan, the lender is likely to allow assumption or a substitution of liability by the new owners. If, however, interest rates have risen, the lender would want the lower rate loan repaid or would give a new loan at prevailing higher rates.

Some people might suggest ways to get around the due-on-sale clauses to take advantage of low interest rate loans, such as unrecorded land contracts. However, it is strongly advised that such methods be avoided. In addition to moral objections, they present undue risks for the purchaser.

There are legitimate ways to get around "due-on-sale" clauses that block assumption of a loan. One way is to contact the lender and offer to accept an interest increase. Lenders will often agree to a rate less than the market rate they are asking for new loans.

PREPAYMENT PENALTIES

Loans that provide for payments of a stated amount "or more" can be repaid without penalty. In the absence of an "or more" clause, prepayment might subject you to a penalty. In a number of states, prepayment can be made in particular situations without penalty. State law might also limit the amount of penalty that can be assessed.

If you intend to pay off a loan in a relatively short time, a loan without a prepayment penalty is probably your best bet, even if its interest rate is higher than other available loans.

BALLOON PAYMENT

A *balloon payment* is a final payment that is more than twice the amount of the loan's regular monthly payment. As an example, we can look at a loan with monthly payments that are based on a 30-year amortization, but that is due and payable in five years. In other words, the entire principal balance outstanding after five years must be paid off. The danger of a balloon payment is that the owner must be able to meet that final payment or obtain new, affordable financing. Otherwise, foreclosure could result. If the balloon payment comes due during a tight money market when interest rates are high, the owner could be in trouble because affordable refinancing of the loan may not be possible.

OWNER FINANCING

In a buyer's market with many sellers and few buyers, sellers are usually willing to help finance buyers. When sellers don't need the cash and mortgage rates are higher than rates for certificates of deposit in which the owners might otherwise park their cash, they may become receptive to the idea of owner financing. This technique of "carrying paper" has definite economic benefits in such circumstances.

Sellers with assumable loans can finance buyers without any problem. If the seller's loan is not assumable, seller financing is still possible. The buyer can obtain a new first mortgage and the seller can *carry back* a second mortgage. With carry-back financing, the seller finances the buyer for all or part of the purchase price with the use of a mortgage or other instrument that secures the finance loan.

Another seller financing method is for the seller to refinance with a new, assumable first mortgage; the buyer can then assume the mortgage and give the seller a second mortgage. With new loans, it is possible for the seller to obtain substantial cash at closing even though the buyer has no down payment.

Deferred Down Payment

With the offer of a small initial down payment and a large down payment at a later date, sellers can often be convinced to carry the financing.

Escalating Interest

An owner who agrees to finance your purchase may agree to a low down payment or no down payment at all if you make an *escalating-interest* offer designed to appeal to the owner's pocketbook. As an example, a purchase contract could provide for 9 percent interest the first year, with a 1 percent increase each year until a maximum of 16 percent interest is reached. The seller is likely to be intrigued with the thought of getting 16 percent interest. You, on the other hand, must realize that refinancing will be necessary within several years or the payments may become unbearable.

Using the Agent's Money

Sellers who have listed their property with an agent, and who will finance a buyer and accept a low down payment (10 percent or less) want enough cash to cover broker commissions and closing costs.

Many agents will agree to accept a commission in the form of a personal note or second mortgage. If the agent is agreeable, you can make a no-down payment offer whereby you, as buyer, agree to accept the obligation for the brokerage commission and the closing costs. Thus, your total immediate expenses will be limited to closing costs.

Manufacturing a Down Payment

Sellers who are willing to finance buyers often want the down payment to ensure against default, rather than because of a need for cash. If you, as the purchaser, own other property, you can provide the seller with this security by *manufacturing paper*. This means you give the seller a second mortgage on the other property as the down payment. The seller now has security in two properties. Although you will make payments on the second mortgage, you have successfully made a purchase without cash.

Use Your Paper

If you are carrying paper on the sale of another property (i.e., you financed a buyer and are carrying back a mortgage), you might want to use this paper in trade for your down payment or even the entire purchase price of another property. If an owner indicates willingness to finance a buyer, the owner simply wants a secure investment with monthly income. If the security on the paper you are carrying is as good as or better than the seller's security on the property you wish to buy, then you should be able to convince the seller to accept your well-secured mortgage for all or part of his or her equity.

Private Loans

If a home has an assumable loan from private individuals (previous owners), it could be wise to assume these loans, even though you are prepared to pay cash or obtain more advantageous new financing. After the purchase, you should contact the holders of the loans and offer to pay them off if they will provide a discount. Because owners like the idea of cash in hand, they will generally agree to at least a 10 percent discount, but 20 percent to 30 percent discounts are often possible. The net effect of this maneuver is to obtain a price reduction after the purchase.

APPLYING FOR A LOAN

You should shop for a loan with as much care as when you shopped for a home. Loan conditions such as assumability and prepayment penalties vary among lenders, as do the initial loan costs, payment periods, and interest rates. What you want is a loan that best meets your individual needs.

Plan to spend some careful time in your search for lenders. Phone calls will give you a great deal of basic information; real estate agents can also be helpful. Some lenders have reputations for being very slow to process loans while others are known for speed and helpfulness. Agents will normally recommend lenders they feel will handle the loan in an expeditious manner.

Before you apply for a loan, a lender will generally *prequalify* you based on your income and expenses. This can be an informal session. Use this time to find about the lending organization and the fees it charges for a loan. Some lenders will give you computer printouts or handwritten worksheets detailing this data; however, fees are subject to change and the rates quoted are usually not guaranteed. Prequalification does not mean you will get the loan, but it could mean that you needn't bother to apply.

Some lenders will take a loan application without an initial fee. The lender's loan committee will then agree to make the loan contingent on your credit report, property appraisal, and verifications of earnings and debts. A fee may be required *after* initial approval.

More likely, your initial loan application will require the payment of an amount ranging from several hundred dollars to around $1,000. Therefore, be selective when applying for loans. Multiple applications with initial fees should generally be avoided.

Be leery of any mortgage company you know little about that seems to offer much better loans than other lenders. The lender might claim to be handling loans for "Eastern," "Western," or even "foreign" investors. Unfortunately, there are many rip-off artists operating in the mortgage business who collect upfront fees for loans that never materialize. If a loan appears too good to be true, stay away from it.

Chapter 8:
Closing, Settlement, and Possession

The completion, or *closing*, of a real estate transaction is the final exchange of the instrument of title (deed) and the buyer's consideration (money and/or mortgages).

CLOSING PROCESS

In states using an escrow (an independent firm that handles closings), the escrowee prepares all documents and handles the entire closing process. The associated costs are customarily split between buyer and seller, although this cost is negotiable. Escrowees prepare escrow instructions to be signed by both buyers and sellers. In the event the escrow instructions are different from the purchase agreement, the escrow instructions govern. Therefore, it is essential that prior to signing escrow instructions, you ascertain that they properly reflect the purchase agreement, and that all conditions are set forth. The escrow will close in accordance with the directions given, and understandings or agreements not set forth in the instructions will have no effect on the closing.

In many areas where escrows are not used, the listing broker prepares a settlement as well as documents of transfer. In other states, all deeds, mortgages, notes, and other pertinent documents are prepared by attorneys.

Closings are attended by the buyer and his or her attorney, the seller (who might also have counsel), the broker (whose attorney might also be present), and, in some cases, the lender's representative. A closing statement prepared by the broker or seller's attorney is reviewed. The deed to the property is given to the buyer, and the seller receives a certified or cashier's check for his or her equity. In cases where loans are paid off, checks are given for that purpose as well. Any new mortgages are given to the new lenders.

Avoid Large Purchases

Prior to closing, some prospective purchasers will make credit purchases of furniture or appliances for their new home. Unfortunately, by doing so, they alter their credit status and their home loan is disapproved. Major credit purchases, such as automobiles and furniture, should be avoided while you are waiting for loan approval on your new home. After the home is purchased, you can assess your capability to assume additional debt; prior to approval, it could be disastrous.

Walk-Through

In many cases, a buyer *walk-through* the premises is performed immediately prior to closing so the buyer can ascertain that all work to be performed has been performed and that what is to be included with the real property has been left on the premises. Sometimes this walk-through is also used to verify that all mechanical, electrical and plumbing equipment, appliances, and systems are in good and proper working condition. It is recommended, however, that these checks be performed well before the final walk-through in order to provide time for any required repairs. Otherwise, closing could be delayed by minor repair requirements.

The Role of the Attorneys

The role of attorneys in real estate closings varies from state to state. Generally, the buyer's attorney checks the title and ascertains that all legal requirements of the transaction have been complied with.

The buyer's attorney also checks any mortgages to be given and determines that the closing statement is correct.

The seller's attorney drafts the deed and any mortgages to be carried back by the seller, if this is not done by the real estate broker or the broker's attorney. The seller's attorney might draft the closing statement, although this is likely to be done by the broker or the broker's attorney if a broker is involved. The seller's attorney would also check to make certain that all conditions of the sale were complied with.

Legal costs for real estate transactions vary tremendously. In some areas of the country, legal fees are based on the sale price; however, most fees are determined by actual or expected time involved. The fees for legal services are generally higher for buyers than for sellers and can range from several hundred dollars to thousands of dollars, depending on the complexity of the transaction and the nature and extent of problems along the way.

Utilities

The seller should arrange for utilities to be taken out of his or her name as of the date of closing. At the same time, the buyer should make certain that utilities will be left on and transferred to him or her. In areas of the country where winters are harsh, extreme damage to pipes and other internal structures is possible if water, electricity, or gas is disconnected.

The buyer should realize that most utility companies require a deposit before the start of service. In some areas of the country, these deposits can be substantial.

Prorating

The seller is generally liable for all expenses up to and including the date of closing. Thus, any amounts prepaid by the buyer for insurance, rents, mortgage payments, and taxes are *prorated*, or assessed proportionately. Prorating is sometimes based on a 30-day month and a 360-day year. In some states, prorating is based on actual calendar days. For example, assume closing for the 15th of February. The property has a tenant and the tenant pays $400 per month rent in advance on the first of each month. Assume also that the buyer is taking on an existing loan and the loan payment is payable on the first of each month; the amount due on March 1 will include $523 in interest for the month of February. The seller is entitled to keep the rent for the first 15 days of the month when he or she had title, but must credit $200 to the buyer for the rent after closing. The buyer will be paying $523 in interest for all of February, even though the seller actually had possession of the property for 15 days of that month. The seller must therefore credit the buyer with $261.50, or half the interest amount paid by the buyer.

Fuel

Normally, the amount of oil in tanks is estimated, and the closing provides for the seller to be credited with its current value. This is no insignificant concern: With current oil prices being what they are, and with the sizes of residential tanks ranging from 250 to 500 gallons, the fuel expense to be paid by the buyer could be substantial.

Insurance

Fire insurance is prepaid. If the buyer assumes a policy from the seller, the seller would be entitled to reimbursement for the prorated value of the unused portion of the insurance.

Before assuming an existing insurance policy, a buyer should ascertain that the current policy provides adequate coverage. If there is to be a new loan on the property, lenders might insist on increased coverage. As a home purchaser, you will probably want a homeowner's policy that includes extended coverage for damage to the property as well as a wide range of personal property and personal liability coverage. All homeowner policies are not the same; review carefully any policy you are considering assuming, keeping your needs and wants in mind. For example:

Does the policy include replacement coverage? Normally, when contents are destroyed, policies provide for current value of the used contents, which is usually only a fraction of the cost to replace them. For a few dollars more, replacement cost coverage will insure you for the cost to *replace* damaged items.

Is the policy a good deal, cost-wise? Get quotes for similar coverage. You may find that costs of policies vary significantly.

Sellers will often want you to assume their policy for an economic reason. If you assume the policy, you will pay them a prorated share of the cost. If, however, you obtained new insurance coverage, the sellers would have to cancel their coverage. When a policy is cancelled, the insurance company returns what is known as a *short rate refund*, which is less than the prorated amount.

Impound Accounts

Impound accounts are accounts kept by the lender for taxes and insurance. In this way the lender is assured that taxes are being paid and the property is insured; the amounts due for these purposes are added to the monthly purchase payments. Although lenders hold these accounts paying little or no interest, the accounts actually belong to the owner. If, upon sale of the property, the property is refinanced, the owner would get back the amount in the impound account. If the property is sold and the loan assumed, the buyer would reimburse the seller for the impound account. (Taxes and insurance would still be prorated upon closing.)

Revenue Stamps

At one time, there was a federal tax on real estate transfers. Federal *documentary transfer tax stamps* were required to be on all deeds and were based on the seller's equity being transferred. When the federal government abandoned this tax, most states saw a source of revenue and adopted it as a tax for state or county revenue. The seller customarily pays for the revenue stamps that are attached to the deed, although in some jurisdictions the buyer is responsible for municipal revenue stamps.

Drafting, Notarization, and Recording

Generally, the party giving a document pays to draft and notarize the document. The party receiving it generally pays to record it.

DEBITS AND CREDITS OF CLOSING

Purchasers often fail to realize all of the direct expenses associated with purchasing, and sellers often don't realize the direct expenses associated with selling. They are surprised when closing statements indicate they must pay more or will get less than they expected.

The following list shows what *credits* and *debits* buyers and sellers can expect on their closing statements. A credit is money you are entitled to (if you are a seller) or a deduction from the purchase money (if you are a buyer). Debits are deductions from the sale price (if you are a seller) or additional monies required (if you are a buyer).

Seller Credits:
- Sale price
- Impound accounts (loans being assumed)
- Prepaid insurance (being assumed)
- Taxes (if prepaid beyond closing date)

Seller Debits:
- Existing loans being assumed by buyer
- New loans accepted as part of purchase price
- Cost of drafting and notarizing deed
- Cost of recording new mortgages received
- Loans being paid off

- Prepayment penalties on loans paid off
- Termite inspection (if agreed to)
- Required termite repairs
- Commission to agent
- Down payment received
- Prepaid rents
- Homeowner warranty insurance (if given by seller)
- Cost of bringing *abstract* (a property's recorded history) up to date
- Standard policy of title insurance (if agreed to be paid by seller)
- Revenue stamps
- Escrow fees (if applicable)
- Any existing tax liens or mechanic's liens against property

The seller is entitled to receive the balance needed for the debits to equal the credits upon closing.

The buyer's closing statement is different from the seller's, and has different credits and debits:

Buyer Credits:
- Down payment given
- Loans being assumed
- New loans to be given seller as part of purchase price
- Other liens against property (tax and mechanic's liens)
- Taxes (if buyer will be paying for taxes for period when seller was in possession)
- Interest (prorated for loans being assumed)

Buyer Debits:
- Sale price
- Extended coverage policy of title insurance (if desired or required by lender)
- Recording cost for deed received
- Tax and insurance reserves
- Fire insurance being assumed
- New loan charges

- Escrow fees (if applicable)
- Prepaid interest for balance of month for new loan

The buyer will have to pay the amount at closing necessary to have the buyer credits equal the buyer debits.

ABSTRACTS AND TITLE INSURANCE

In many areas *abstract checks* by attorneys are the common method to verify that the seller has a marketable title. An abstract is a recorded history of a property. It contains copies of all recorded documents concerning a property, and can often run several hundred pages in length. Abstracts are prepared by abstract companies. When property that has a recorded history is sold, the abstract firm updates the abstract. An abstract company generally does not warrant title. It does, however, warrant that all properly recorded documents dealing with the property have been reported.

An attorney reading the abstract would look for liens and encumbrances that were not subsequently removed, and for inconsistencies that could affect the title. Based on the examination, the attorney will give an *opinion of title*, subject to stated exceptions.

The seller generally pays to update the abstract, while the buyer normally carries the responsibility to pay for legal advice regarding the title's marketability.

The abstract provides no buyer protection for forgery of a deed or release of a lien. From the abstract, you cannot ascertain that a person signing a document had legal or mental capacity to sign. *An abstract only shows that items were recorded; delivery of marketable title, however, is required, and while recording might presume delivery, this presumption could be overcome.* There could also be unrecorded tax liens or unknown spousal interests that abstracts would not disclose. Therefore, there are weaknesses in a title opinion based on an abstract. However, a buyer would be protected from the above defects in a title with a standard policy of *title insurance*. Because it offers greater protection, title insurance is slowly replacing abstracts as the means to verify title. Generally, the seller pays for the standard title insurance policy. Title insurance protects only the person insuring the title, so a buyer would not get title protection for a title defect that was covered by an insurance policy issued to a previous owner.

The standard title insurance policy does not offer protection against parties in possession who might have rights under an unrecorded valid lease or a lease with option to purchase. Also not covered are mechanic's rights to file liens for work on the premises, unrecorded easements (rights of way across property), or claims that might result from a correct survey. It is possible that improvements were placed on the wrong lot or that a building encroaches onto the lot of another. Mining claims and water rights are also not protected by a standard policy of title insurance.

Extended coverage for the above is available at additional cost, which is generally paid for by the buyer. Lenders often require that the borrower protect them with extended title coverage.

Title insurance does not protect an owner against changes in zoning, although it is possible to purchase an endorsement that stipulates zoning at the time of the coverage. Title insurance also does not cover defects known by the insured but not disclosed to the insurance company.

POSSESSION

If possession is given to the purchasers prior to closing, the purchasers could be liable for risk of loss. (Normally in a sale transaction, risk transfers with possession.) Therefore, the purchasers should make certain they are adequately insured.

Although a common practice, it's often dangerous for sellers to give buyers possession prior to closing. Being in possession prior to closing increases the likelihood that the prospective buyers will find something they are not happy with and will want corrected. In addition, should a dispute arise between the parties, the purchaser could conceivably remain in possession of the property without paying for occupancy for as long as the dispute lasts. Sellers wishing to protect themselves should have a written month-to-month lease with the buyers, clearly showing that the buyers are tenants only and subject to legal notice to vacate. In all events, if possession is to be given prior to a closing it is recommended that legal advice be secured.

Although possession is usually granted immediately upon closing the sales transaction, this does present a potential problem. If possession is to be given upon closing, the seller will obviously have to vacate beforehand, and either rent or buy another property. If, for some reason, the sale falls through, the seller could end up with a vacant house as well as a house he is obligated to rent or purchase. The result is two house payments. Furthermore, vacant property is more difficult to sell than a well-maintained furnished home.

Some advisers suggest possession be set at 30 days after closing, with a provision that the seller would pay rent to the buyer for the period from closing until transfer of possession. Be aware, however, that some advisers and attorneys require a transfer of possession the day of closing.

Chapter 9:
Your Investment—
Upgrades and Collateral

Many people make repairs, renovate, and remodel their homes with no concern for the effect of their efforts on resale. True, a home is very personal, and some investments and improvements are made strictly for comfort and enjoyment; their value is in their use, not in what they add to price upon resale. However, most improvements will be reflected in the sales price when your property is sold. Some improvements will result in a return, at the time of sale, of an amount greater than cost; others will return less. How others perceive the improvement's desirability will determine its effect on sales price.

RESTORATION

Restoration is a return to an original condition. Restoration might be considered for older homes of classic design. As an example, in the 1940s and 1950s, many owners of Victorian homes removed the gingerbread wood trim because it was considered old-fashioned. The resurgence of interest in Victorian homes would likely make restoration of such a home a sound economic investment.

RENOVATION

Renovation is simply repairs. It is an ongoing process. Seriously neglected homes, when renovated, often have resale values that far exceed their cost plus the cost of renovation. These "fixer-uppers" can offer exceptional opportunity for the home purchaser.

REMODELING

Remodeling means changing. Remodeling frequently requires a building permit; keep in mind that the value of the remodeled house can be reflected in your property tax base.

REGRESSION

In making any repairs or improvements, keep in mind the principle of regression (see Chapter 4). If you make your home better than all of your neighbors' homes, the lower value of your neighbors' properties will have a negative effect on the value of your home. It would not be economical to put a $50,000 addition on a $40,000 home in an area of $40,000 to $50,000 homes. A more economical decision would be to sell the property and buy or build a $90,000 home in an area of higher-valued homes.

TYPICAL HOME IMPROVEMENTS

Kitchen Remodeling
The attractiveness of the kitchen follows location in importance to homebuyers. While a complete professional kitchen remodeling job would be unlikely to be fully reflected in resale value, except in very expensive homes, kitchen remodeling of a lesser nature is likely to be an economically viable improvement. A good time to remodel is when appliances are being replaced. Some of the work to consider would include:

- New countertops
- New sinks and/or faucets
- New vinyl or ceramic flooring
- Refinished or refaced cabinetry
- New lighting fixtures
- New wall coverings

Bath Addition and Remodeling

Adding a second bath to a single-bath home is generally a wise economic improvement. On average, a bath addition will cost a homeowner $8,000. However, the average difference in value between one- and two-bath homes of similar size is $10,000. This gives a homeowner a 25 percent profit (based on increased sale value) for a bath addition.

Bath remodeling will frequently make a great deal of sense from an economic viewpoint. Ceramic floor and wall tile, new built-in vanity sinks and hardware as well as tasteful lighting can turn a lackluster bathroom into an extremely strong feature of your home when it is time for resale.

Room Additions

It is seldom that the cost of room additions to a home will be fully reflected in increased selling price. In cases where the addition does not blend in with the floor plan and/or the architecture, the net effect of an addition could actually be an overall lower value. Bedroom additions will return a higher percentage of their cost than will family room additions.

Enclosing existing porches to increase usability will generally have a positive effect on value, although the total cost might not be recoverable upon resale.

Basement Rooms

Basement rooms do not contribute as much to value as would the addition of first- or second-floor space. However, basement rooms can be finished at an extremely low price per square foot. Where the basement is, or can be, exposed to allow for large windows or sliding glass doors, the conversion to living space will have a more positive effect on value than a basement that offers more limited natural lighting.

Swimming Pools and Tennis Courts

In some very warm areas of the country, the addition of a swimming pool or tennis court will be fully reflected in the sale price when the home is sold. The likelihood that the cost of a pool or tennis court will be fully recoverable upon sale increases with the value of the property. For example, a $15,000 pool cost would more likely be recoverable on the sale of a $200,000 home than a $60,000 home. In other areas of the country, the presence of a pool will not increase the sale price significantly.

Garages

When a property does not have a garage, the addition of a garage—especially an oversized, double garage—is likely to have an effect on value as great or greater than its cost. When a property already has a garage, the cost of adding another garage is unlikely to be recoverable upon resale.

Attic and Garage Conversion

Conversion of attic space to usable rooms by means of dormers will generally have a positive effect on value because the space can be made usable at relatively low cost per square foot.

On the other hand, the cost of converting garages to living space would unlikely be fully reflected in the sale price. The reason is that the space appears to be just what it is: a garage turned into a room.

Fireplaces

Installing a fireplace to an existing home costs an average of about $3,500, yet it adds an average value of about $4,500. So, in terms of pure economics, a fireplace addition is a wise home improvement to make.

Central Air

Central air-conditioning can be readily added to most modern forced-air furnaces and is generally an excellent home improvement. Not only does it improve the quality of life, it increases the resale value of a home. For homes sold during a hot summer period, the presence of central air can increase the sale price in excess of what it cost to install the air-conditioning. Lowest installation costs are available during the winter months.

Roof Repair and Replacement

Roof repair and/or replacement is necessary if the roof leaks. However, a new roof is not an economic investment. Its cost is unlikely to be fully returned in the increased resale value.

Siding

A principal advantage of aluminum or vinyl siding is low maintenance costs. It can also be used to hide many problems. Installation costs vary widely, depending on the installer and the material selected. When existing siding is in bad shape, the cost of new siding may be returned in the sale price. However, where aluminum or vinyl siding is installed over good wood siding, primarily to reduce maintenance, the cost of the siding is unlikely to be recaptured in the sale price.

Be aware that many siding and home remodeling contractors use high-pressure sales tactics and charge prices that reflect higher than normal markups. You should obtain competitive bids on major work using comparable specifications. Contractors should understand that other bids will be sought.

Storm Windows and Screens

Aluminum self-storing storm windows and screens that are permanently installed over existing windows are available in most standard sizes for homeowner installation. Economically, they make sense in colder climates for savings on energy costs. However, the cost of the installation is unlikely to be recoverable in the home's sale price.

Insulation

In homes that have attic or ceiling space, additional ceiling insulation can be a wise investment. While it will have little effect on resale value, it can provide heating and cooling cost savings that will return the investment in only a few years. Additional insulation can be blown in or be installed in batts. In some areas, utility companies give rebates for installing additional insulation; some states offer tax credits for energy conservation efforts.

Roof Vents

Many older homes have poor attic space ventilation. In summer, the dead air space becomes extremely hot, increasing cooling costs and making the house uncomfortable. Roof vents are inexpensive and are very effective in reducing the temperature in the dead air space. Some vents operate on a wind turbine basis, but a power vent with thermostat will cost around $100 and can easily be installed in a dormer by a homeowner. Vents installed in the roof itself should generally be professionally handled.

Heating Conversions

Electric heat is a negative feature in many areas of the country because of rising electric costs. Large homes with electric heat and high electric bills tend to discourage would-be buyers. Such a home can often be purchased at a substantial discount from the value it would have if it were heated by natural gas. The installation of a baseboard hot water heating system from a natural gas-fired boiler is often an economically sound investment. Not only will heating costs be reduced, the sale price will likely reflect a value in excess of the cost of the system.

In more rural, snowbelt areas, where bottled gas or oil is used for heat and firewood is readily available at a low cost, an add-on wood furnace can be an economic investment.

For old furnaces that were converted to oil or gas, a modern furnace replacement would likely be an economic investment. In addition to greater efficiency, the cost is likely to be largely reflected in the sale price and ease of sale.

Solar Panels

Solar heat panels may save energy to some extent, but as a whole, they do not make economic sense when you compare the cost for professional installation and the energy savings that are likely. Though special state tax credits can make solar installations a viable investment, the cost of a solar heating installation is unlikely to be recaptured in the home's sale price.

Greenhouse Addition

A quality greenhouse addition to a very expensive home is likely to result in a price at the time of resale that exceeds the cost of the addition. This type of addition, however, is unlikely to be a good economic investment for middle- and lower-cost housing.

Security Features

Steel awnings, bars on windows, steel doors and jambs, and other security features are expensive. They may contribute to peace of mind, but seldom do they add anything of value when the time comes to sell. In fact, the presence of excessive security features can actually scare away many prospective purchasers.

Professional Landscaping

Professional landscaping projects are expensive, but they make economic sense for more expensive homes. Generally, the more expensive the home, the greater the effect professional landscaping will have on value. The more mature the trees and plants, the greater the expense of landscaping. Considerable savings are possible with younger but fast-growing trees and shrubs.

As an alternative to professional landscaping, many nurseries as well as landscape architects will prepare a detailed landscape plan for a fee. By doing much of the work yourself, you will gain a personal feeling of accomplishment, and you will realize significant savings as well.

HOME MAINTENANCE

Proper home maintenance reduces the likelihood of expensive repairs, and it helps maintain a home's value. Considering the cost of your home, it deserves to be properly maintained.

When something is not working properly, it should be repaired. Putting off small tasks tends to increase the likelihood of major work.

Monthly maintenance should consist of simply changing the filter on your furnace and/or air conditioner. When these appliances are not receiving much use, this can be done every few months.

A semiannual spring and fall inspection of your home should be done and maintenance performed when required. Items to be checked include:

- *Caulking.* Check around windows and doors, and where the house joins the foundation for needed caulking or repairs to caulking.
- *Weatherstripping.* Check around doors and windows to see if the weatherstripping needs to be replaced.
- *Toilets.* Check for gurgling toilets that need tank adjustment or repair.
- *Faucets.* Replace washers and/or reseat faucets that drip.
- *Water heater.* Connect a hose to the outlet on the bottom of tank and drain off any sediment that may have accumulated.
- *Furnace/Air conditioner.* If your fan motor has an oil cap, a few drops of oil should be added. Belts should be checked for tightness.
- *Gutters.* Clean gutters and run a hose to clear downspouts of debris.

- *Rot.* Check exterior wood trim closest to the ground, including porches and stairs, for rot. Use a penknife to poke at wood. Replace any rotted boards. If there is a crawlspace, check beneath the space for dry rot.
- *Termites.* Check inside the foundation and in your bathtub's plumbing-access panel for signs of termites or carpenter ants. Signs include granules of dust-like material, dirt tunnels, and hollowed-out boards.
- *Other insects.* Check under sinks for roaches. They can also be discovered by simply turning on the kitchen lights in the middle of the night and looking at the floor for fast-moving small objects.
- *Rodents.* Check the foundation for cracks where rodents can enter; check for droppings in less accessible areas. If you find evidence of rodents, use commercial poisons and/or traps, or contact an exterminator.

BORROWING ON YOUR HOME: COLLATERAL

In terms of value, the average American's greatest single asset is the *equity* in his or her home. Equity is the difference between what your home is worth and any amounts owed against it. What you will net from a sale is not the same as your equity. Sales commissions and associated costs will reduce your net.

To tap your equity, you don't have to wait until you sell your home; you can borrow money using your home as collateral. There are many good reasons to borrow: home improvements, children's educations, medical expenses, investments, business needs, and even debt consolidation.

Deductibility and Credit Limits

Interest on the first $100,000 of a home equity loan is tax deductible; the loan can be used for any purpose. If the loan is used for home improvements, interest on any loan amount up to $1,000,000 may be deducted.

Due to recent tax law changes, interest on credit card loans and loans not secured by your home are no longer deductible after the phase-in periods contained in the Tax Reform Act of 1986. Therefore it would be a sound economic decision to pay off these loans with a home loan. In addition to the possibility of deducting interest, home loans have lower interest rates than general consumer loans and credit cards. There is a problem, however, in using a collateralized home loan to pay off consumer loans: By paying off these loans, the homeowner now has a high credit limit. To many, this is an invitation to spend. Thus, the wisdom of using a home loan to pay off consumer credit depends largely on the self-control of the borrower. Where self-control is lacking, the result could be new debt in addition to the home loan. *The ready availability of home loans and heavy advertising of them have caused many homeowners to lose their home equity because of frivolous spending.* Remember how important your home is to you; *never take on a home equity loan for any but the most sensible reasons.*

Refinancing

Refinancing a first mortgage or arranging a new second mortgage both involve loan costs such as appraisal fees, title searches, title insurance, and points. Keep in mind that to borrow on your home requires you to pay back a greater principal amount than you receive, since these costs will be added to your loan.

When you refinance, an existing loan is replaced by a new loan at a greater amount. The excess amount above and beyond costs is then given to the borrower. A second mortgage leaves the existing home loan intact. The homeowner now has two loan payments to make.

First mortgages generally have a lower rate of interest than junior mortgages because of the lower risk to the lender. However, refinancing to obtain a new first mortgage could mean abandoning an attractive rate of interest for a higher rate. The borrower should carefully analyze loan costs as well as total interest costs when making a decision to refinance. One alternative is to keep the old loan and get a second mortgage at a higher rate.

Chapter 10:
Selling Your Home

Homes are sold for a variety of reasons—some voluntary, some involuntary. A home may no longer meet its owners' needs, or the owners may desire to relocate. Perhaps the sale is mandated by a divorce decree, or the owners have to sell to avoid foreclosure. Perhaps a job transfer necessitates relocation. Whatever the case, the reason for sale can affect both sale price and terms.

DISINCENTIVE TO SELL

In states such as California, where homes are reassessed for property taxes only upon sale, there is a disincentive to sell. A sale of a home having low taxes could result in taxes on a new, less valuable home being dramatically higher. In many cases, the purchase of a new home of the same value could mean a doubling or even tripling of taxes.

AN AGENT

You can sell your home without an agent, and many people do so successfully. However, most owners who try to sell their homes themselves end up engaging an agent.

The primary reason most sellers employ an agent is simple: It's the route most buyers take. Think back to when you were a buyer. It's likely you went to agents because agents control a part of the market through their listings and have access to a great many more properties through a multiple-listing service. Chances are you went to an agent because to do so was the most practical way to buy a home. It was far easier to assess the market and find a home that meets your needs by dealing through one or several agents than to look for "For Sale By Owner" signs or answer ads that were often misleading. Buyers today are not any different than when you were a buyer. Most serious buyers do contact agents.

FOR SALE BY OWNER

There are times when the likelihood of successfully selling your own home will be increased tremendously. These times are during a seller's market, when there are many buyers and few sellers. In such a market, serious buyers will cruise streets looking for any "For Sale" signs. They will also answer "For Sale By Owner" ads.

Yet for the most part, many owners are not temperamentally prepared to deal directly with buyers. They feel insulted at any criticism directed at their property. Too, buyers feel uncomfortable dealing with owners; it's easier to work with a more neutral third party, such as a broker. For example, if a buyer feels a price offered for a home by a broker is too high, he or she is likely to say so and a buyer offer is possible. This type of response is less likely when the buyer deals directly with the owner; in fact, the buyer is apt to dismiss altogether the property as a possible purchase.

Of course, the primary reason owners try to sell property themselves is to avoid the broker's commission.

PREQUALIFICATION

Many owners waste a great deal of time with unqualified buyers who, because of insufficient income, credit problems, or excessive loan payments, couldn't possibly qualify for the required home loan. The reason is that owners are reluctant to ask pointed questions about a person's ability to buy before an offer has been extended. As an owner, don't get excited over any buyer until he or she has signed a contract, given a significant down payment, and has been qualified for any required financing. An advantage of listing with an agent is that most agents prequalify a buyer's financial ability.

PRICING

If you are a serious seller, you should price your home at what similar properties are actually *selling* for, not at what they were listed for. Pricing closer to market value will result in a quicker sale. Studies have shown that the higher properties are priced over market prices, the longer the time required to sell. Other studies seem to indicate the actual sale prices of similar homes listed at and above market value do not materially differ.

PREPARING YOUR HOME FOR SALE

When you place your home on the market, you are putting it into competition with every other home on the market, including homes that are brand-new. You want your home to compare favorably with homes in the same general price bracket because, effectively, that is where your competition exists. How do you get the edge on the competition? There are a number of relatively inexpensive things you can do:

Landscaping

A quick-greening fertilizer, such as ammonium sulfate, can give you the greenest lawn in the neighborhood. Plant grass or sod where needed, and keep plants well-trimmed. If you have a dog, clean the lawn on a daily basis.

Flowers set in beds in the front of the house and around the patio can have a tremendously positive effect on prospective buyers. The cost will be less than $100.

If you need them, plant trees and shrubs. Bare-root plants are available at low cost. Fruit trees, even small ones, are well regarded by prospective buyers.

Consider adding a bird feeder, several bird houses, and a hummingbird feeder in the backyard. For very few dollars, they add a special touch to a home.

Exterior

If the exterior of your home needs to be painted, now is the time to do it or have it done. Often it is only the trim that needs paint, or perhaps only one or two sides of the house.

Fences and gates should be in good repair. Paint if needed.

The front door should be painted, varnished, or polished as required. A new brass knocker can be a nice inexpensive touch.

Exterior lighting fixtures should be cleaned. Too, consider a new oversized lighting fixture for the front of your home. Low-voltage, front-yard lights are relatively inexpensive and give a nice touch, especially in the winter months when your home is likely to be viewed after dark.

Garage and Basement

The garage and basement should be cleaned up. Things you want to save should be put into boxes and piled neatly in a basement corner or in the garage rafters. As an alternative, consider renting self-storage space. Cluttered areas tend to look small.

Interior

Your carpeting should be clean. Even worn carpeting will appear more attractive with a good cleaning. You can rent a steam cleaner at many chain supermarkets, or you can use the services of a professional carpet cleaner.

Some homeowners frequently change carpeting when they redecorate, even though the carpeting does not show any wear. Carpet-layers will normally save this carpeting. If your carpet is badly worn, consider contacting carpet-layers to ask about used carpeting they may have. Frequently, they will sell this carpeting at a nominal price.

If you have matching paint, interior walls can be touched up where needed. If the walls require more work, stretch the job out over several weekends. Use a good latex flat wall paint in the living room, halls, and bedrooms, and a latex semigloss paint in the kitchen and bath. Use light colors (off-white, cream, or a light buff); this will make the rooms appear larger.

Consider judicious use of wallpaper and/or paneling; the effect can be extremely positive.

Clean all blinds, drapes, and windows. Water marks on windows can be removed with a good commercial calcium-and-lime remover.

Appliances and porcelain should be cleaned and polished. An autowax can be used. Floor and wall tile should also sparkle.

Many people have a lot of furniture and bric-a-brac. Too much furniture or overpoweringly large pieces will make rooms seem small. Consider using a storage facility.

Replace low-wattage bulbs with higher wattage. You want your house to appear as bright as possible.

Clean all interior lighting fixtures. A nondescript kitchen, bath, dining area, or hall can convey a strong positive image with a new, tasteful lighting fixture.

Very often, dollars spent in sprucing up a home for resale will multiply themselves tenfold in the sale price, as well as shorten the time necessary to bring about a sale.

PROMOTING YOUR HOME

When you sell a home without an agent, you must plan on promoting it yourself. In addition to a "For Sale By Owner" sign that includes a phone number, you want to let your relatives, friends, work acquaintances, and even your religious leader know you are selling your home.

If you live close to a major traffic artery or to a new development that offers open houses, open-house arrows to your home and open-house signs on weekends will direct traffic to your home without using ads.

If you do plan to use classified ads to promote your home, here are a few general rules:

- Don't repeat the same classified ad constantly. Rewrite the ad on a regular basis, emphasizing different features each time. This will attract the greatest number of prospective buyers.
- Include the asking price in the ad. Many prospective buyers will not call on an unpriced ad.
- If the location is a positive feature of your home and is not indicated by the newspaper advertising category, put it in the ad.
- Whenever possible, the heading should indicate a desirable feature such as:

4 Bedrooms
Oakdale—$49,000 (two features)
Zoned for horses
No down payment
Dutch Colonial

- Avoid too many abbreviations. They make ads difficult to read.

From your ads and signs, you can expect calls from agents, some of whom might indicate they have a buyer. As a word of caution, know that some of these prospective buyers may be real but others are imaginary; the agent may be primarily interested in a listing.

For agents who do have real buyers, you might want to sign an *open listing* that gives the agent the equivalent of a one-half split commission if the buyer is interested. This would be equal to what the agent would receive if he or she sold a home listed by another agent.

PURCHASER SCAMS

As a seller, please realize that there are people who dream up ingenious schemes designed to steal your property or pay you less for it than you think you are getting. Normally, these types of purchasers concentrate their efforts on owners selling without an agent. Con artists tend to avoid agents because agents have a duty to protect their principal, the owner.

Some of the recent scams include:

- *Trading colored gems or uncut diamonds for a seller's equity.* The buyer usually provides an appraisal of the stones that indicates higher value than the seller was hoping for from the house. Even when the appraisal accurately reflects the stones' retail value, the amount that the homeowner could realize on the wholesale market would be far less than the retail value indicated. This is especially true of colored gems. However, in many cases, the appraisals submitted bear no relationship to true retail value. The result usually is loss of a home for a handful of pretty stones of questionable value.

- *Subordination.* A number of seminar presenters have been advocating subordination as a means of buying without any cash, as well as a means to be a purchaser and end up with cash in the pocket. While the seminar presenters don't advocate perpetrating fraud on sellers, their students can see the opportunity to make money quickly at the expense of others.

  Typically, a buyer will present an offer to purchase with a significant cash down payment, if the seller will agree to carry the balance, usually for a year, at a high interest rate. Sellers who are singled out for this scam usually own their homes free and clear, or have only a small existing mortgage. The purchase offer is often at the seller's full asking price and the seller is delighted with it.

However, unnoticed or not understood is the use of the word "subordinate" in the purchase agreement. The seller agrees to carry back a subordinate mortgage. The buyer is then able to refinance the property, relegating the seller's carry-back loan to a junior encumbrance in order to end up with cash. The buyer will not make payments on any of the loans, causing the property to be foreclosed.

To illustrate the above, assume Adam wants to sell his home for $200,000. Also, assume that Adam owes $50,000 on a mortgage. Baker approaches Adam and offers $200,000 for the home, agreeing to pay Adam $50,000 cash and assume the $50,000 loan. Baker agrees to give Adam a $100,000 subordinate mortgage at 13 percent, all due and payable in one year. Adam thinks that it is too good to be true and accepts the offer. Baker obtains a new $150,000 first mortgage. Baker then pays off the $50,000 loan, gives Adam $50,000, and has $50,000 cash in his pocket. But Baker does not make any payments on the $150,000 loan and the lender forecloses. The only way for Adam to protect what equity he has left is to make the payments for Baker and foreclose on his "subordinate" loan.

- *"No Down Payment."* This purchaser swindle has been common in buyers' markets, where there are many sellers and few buyers. In cases where a homeowner has an assumable loan, the purchaser agrees to assume the loan and pay in cash the balance of the purchase price, usually at the asking price, within a short period of time. The seller is to be secured by a second mortgage. The buyer generally indicates he has another home that recently sold, and that he will be getting the cash in a few months when the sale closes. As is the case with the subordination scam, the sellers think this is a great deal for them; unfortunately, it doesn't work out that way. The buyer immediately rents the home and fails to make payments on the assumed loan. The buyer usually has a great many excuses for the owner and lender and gets several months behind before foreclosure begins. If the first mortgage forecloses, the seller's equity (second mortgage) is wiped out. The seller might cure the default and foreclose on the second mortgage to save his equity. In either case, the purchaser collects rent prior to foreclosure and during the foreclosure process. There are recorded cases where individuals have purchased over 100 homes using this technique. The economics of the fraud are simple—ten homes times $400 per month rent equals $4,000 per month clear profit for the purchaser.

- *Trading mortgages.* When sellers indicate a willingness to finance buyers, some purchasers will offer to trade what appear to be well-secured mortgages for an owner's equity. The buyers will generally furnish appraisals indicating the mortgage is well-secured. (Most states do not have standards for appraisals.) In fact, the security for the mortgage being traded is likely to be illusory. For example, a scam artist might buy a parcel of remote land for $10,000. Then he or she will purport to sell the property for $300,000 with $150,000 cash down payment, and a high-interest first mortgage for the balance. In fact, the purchaser was a cohort who paid nothing down; the first mortgage given by the cohort was really manufactured to appear well-secured. Copies of the purchase contract coupled with an appraisal would entice a home seller into giving valuable property for the near-worthless paper. The home seller would not receive payments on the mortgage and would be forced to foreclose, ending up with land having little value. Chances are, the purchaser and mortgagor will have disappeared after selling or borrowing on the property.

- *Taking the impound account.* As noted in Chapter 8, the impound account is an amount kept by the lender to pay taxes and insurance premiums. The account belongs to the seller. At the time of sale, the seller is entitled to a credit for the impound account. The taxes and insurance are then prorated as of the date of closing. Some purchasers have used language such as the following in their purchase agreements: "Purchaser shall assume and take ownership and responsibility of seller's impound account without prorating and without any additional cost or obligation to the seller. Cost of taxes and insurance shall be prorated as of date of closing."

What the buyer's offer really says is, "Give me your impound account and I will give you nothing for it." This amounts to deceit, since the seller, because of language used, does not understand that he is giving something away.

The above are only a few of the many tricks that unscrupulous buyers have been known to use. If a buyer provides his or her own purchase forms that are not standard, offers anything you do not fully understand, or gives an offer that seems too good to be true, see an attorney prior to acceptance.

CREDIT CHECK

If, as a seller, you are to carry back paper on a sale, such as a second mortgage, you want to ascertain the purchaser's credit worthiness. A buyer who has a history of being constantly late on payments can be the source of much aggravation. A buyer who defaults on payments can mean a lengthy and expensive foreclosure process. Some buyers fight foreclosure actions, claiming misrepresentation; thus you could conceivably end up paying off a buyer to give up possession of your property.

You can avoid nightmarish situations such as these with a credit check. Have the buyer obtain his or her credit information for you. This will be on a computer printout. In addition, you should verify the buyer's earnings and employment with his or her employer. If a buyer is a renter, check with prior landlords about any payment problems.

Another way to qualify the purchaser is to ask for several personal references. Call the references and ask for the names of several *other* people who know the purchaser. Now call these parties and ask your questions. You want to know about the purchaser's credit reputation, ethical reputation, whether or not he or she has been involved in any lawsuits, and if so, the nature of the lawsuits.

BE PREPARED

If you elect to sell your home without an agent, be prepared to answer questions about the house. You should know the exact size of your property, taxes, costs of insurance and utilities, and the like. With regard to financing, know whether or not your current loan is assumable as well as interest rates, loan costs, and terms for available loans.

Have several copies of a purchase contract form available, having first familiarized yourself with its terms and conditions. These forms are available at most large stationery supply stores. If there are any state-mandated seller disclosures with regard to known defects and/or seller financing, know what they are and be prepared to make them. Your attorney can help make certain that you comply with specific state statutes.

ASK FOR AN OFFER

A problem faced by many people who attempt to sell their homes themselves is that they have a reluctance to ask lookers to become buyers. They fail to try to close a sale. They are pleasant, they show the house, they offer information, they answer questions, and then they say good-bye.

If you are selling a home yourself, don't be afraid to ask someone to buy. After showing the property and giving price and financing information, ask the potential buyer if he or she liked your home. If the potential buyer responds positively, ask, "Are you considering buying it?" While some prospects may be taken aback by this direct approach, it will motivate others to actually think about buying your house. If the prospect seems receptive, offer him or her purchase forms. While you will encounter a great many "We'll-have-to-think-about-it" responses, a direct approach will increase your chances of sale far more than no sales approach at all.

VERBAL OFFERS

Owners who sell without agents are often approached with verbal offers. A verbal contract for the sale of real estate is generally unenforceable; therefore, you want offers in writing. An appropriate response to a verbal offer is, "If you will put that offer in writing, I'll consider it." Or, you could say, "Make that offer in writing at $(amount) or (other terms) and I will seriously consider it." Have purchase forms ready to give to any prospective buyer. You can fill them out partially in advance with your name, a description of the property, what is included with the property, and other pertinent information.

CHOOSING AN AGENT

Don't choose an agent because a friend or a friend of a friend works at that office. Instead, determine first which realty firms you want to work with. To narrow your decision, use the following criteria:

- *Active in the geographical area where your home is located.* By driving through your neighborhood, you can quickly determine the three or four firms that have the largest number of properties for sale in your area.
- *Quality of advertising.* Check the local papers, especially weekend editions, for the advertising of the firms active in your area.

After deciding on realty firms with which you want to work, contact the firms' brokers and tell them you are considering listing your home for sale. Ask the brokers to make an appointment with one of their most successful salespeople.

You should hold discussions with several agents before you make a listing decision. In making your final decision, keep the following in mind:

- *Professionalism.* The agent must be able to justify the suggested list price with relevant comparable sale prices. Don't give a listing to an agent because the agent says he or she can get a higher price. Quoting unsubstantiated high prices to gain a listing is known as "buying a listing." The agent will usually later try to get the price reduced.

  Be leery of agents who tear down their competitors rather than sell themselves based on what they can do.

- *Compatibility.* You want an agent you feel comfortable working with as well as one you can trust.

- *The agent's firm.* You want a successful firm with few, if any, part-time salespeople. Part-time salespeople are not usually as successful as full-time salespeople, and may lose some good prospects. You want a firm that has a good record with regard to the percentage of listings sold during original-listing periods when compared with multiple-listing service averages. You also want a listing agent and firm that sell a higher than average percentage of their own listings. You don't want to list with a firm that encourages someone else to sell; you want the firm and agent to work for the sale themselves. You might also be interested in the relationship between a firm's list and sale prices average to the average list and sale prices achieved by the local Board of Realtors. When a firm compares favorably with the average, it will generally have the facts to indicate that this is the case.

LISTINGS

By definition, *listings* are agency contracts in which the principal (owner) employs an agent (broker) to procure a buyer. Listings fall into three basic categories: *open listings, exclusive agency listings,* and *exclusive right-to-sell listings.*

Open Listing
Under an *open listing*, the agent is granted a non-exclusive right-to-sell. If an agent procures a buyer who is ready, willing, and able to buy under the terms of the listing, or under any terms the owner agrees to accept, then the agent has earned a commission. If, however, the sale is procured by any other agent or by the owner, then the agent is not entitled to a commission. Multiple open listings can be given to a number of firms at the same time. A sale would cancel the other open listings.

Agents seldom advertise an open listing, since a sale by the owner or by any other agent means no commission. Many real estate offices will not accept open listings.

Exclusive Agency Listings
Under an *exclusive agency listing*, if the listing agent or any other agent sells the property, then the listing agent is entitled to a commission. If, however, the owner sells the property, then the agent is not entitled to a commission. This type of listing can result in problems when it comes to determining whether or not the listing agent was the procuring cause of the sale. Many offices will not accept these listings, since they tend to encourage the owner to compete with the broker.

Exclusive Right-To-Sell Listings
Most listings are *exclusive right-to-sell listings.* Under these arrangements, if the listing broker, any other agent, or the owner sells the property during the listing, then the listing broker earns a commis-

sion. If the property is sold by another agent, that agent also receives a commission.

Safety Clause

Exclusive listings generally have *safety clauses* that protect the agent from having the owner and a prospective buyer delay purchase until after the listing expires. The safety clause provides that should the agent give the owner the names of prospective buyers prior to expiration of the listing, the owner will be obligated to pay a commission if the owner concludes a sale within a stated period of time after expiration (such as ninety days).

Net Listings

Net listings can be exclusive or open listings; the reference is to the commission. With this arrangement, the broker receives all sums over a stated amount (net to owner) as commission. Net listings should be avoided. While you, as owner, want a quick sale and your net amount, the agent wants a sale for as much as possible over the net amount. Therefore, your interests are not really the same. In addition, if the net price is too low, there is the possibility that the agent has not really represented you. Because of past problems, net listings are now illegal in several states. In states where they are legal, many brokers consider them unethical and will not accept them. Be leery of any suggestion of a net listing.

Cooperative Brokerage

In most areas of the country, the majority of sales are made through a *cooperative brokerage*. This means the selling agent is not from the listing firm. Through multiple-listing agreements, agents agree to cooperate with each other and split commissions.

Reduced Commission

Some agents will offer a reduced commission in exchange for a listing. Owners themselves also try to negotiate reduced commission. For the most part, however, a cut-rate listing is a bad bargain. When you list your home at less than the market commission rate, you are putting your property at a competitive disadvantage relative to other properties on the market. Assume you are an agent and have the opportunity to show several properties, one of which is listed at a reduced commission. Which property are you going to be least likely to show? A seller's likelihood of sale is significantly lessened when he or she lists for a reduced commission. A broker who agrees to such an arrangement is not really doing you a favor. In fact, if you were a highly motivated seller, you might consider offering a commission that is *higher* than normal. This is likely to motivate an agent to show your property, giving it a competitive edge.

There is a time when commission reduction should be considered. When you receive an offer for less than list price, you could agree to accept the offer with a reduced commission as opposed to rejecting it or countering it with another offer. Be aware, though, that some brokerage firms will not reduce a commission under any circumstances.

Retaining Your Prospects

Assume you have decided to give an exclusive right-to-sell listing. Assume also you have several prospective buyers who seem interested but have yet to make offers. In this case, you can still give an exclusive right-to-sell listing, excluding your named prospects for a period of time, such as two weeks. After giving such a listing, you should get back to your prospects and tell them you have given an exclusive right-to-sell listing at (dollar amount), but their names have been excluded from the listing for (time period). If they are at all interested, you continue, they can buy the property now at the list price, less commission, an opportunity that will allow them to save (dollar amount). This approach is highly effective with truly interested buyers because the opportunity to avoid paying a broker's commission is a strong lure. An advantage to you is that this approach usually results in a full-price offer. Normally, offers received by brokers are for less than the list price, and the commission is then deducted from the reduced gross sale price.

CONTINGENCY OFFERS

If an offer to purchase your property contains any contingency (see Chapter 6), you want to arrange a time period for compliance, after which the offer shall expire. Otherwise, your property could be off the market for months with no assurance that the sale will go through.

If a buyer extends an offer contingent on VA financing, be aware that your acceptance could obligate you to pay points (see "Loan Points and Costs," Chapter 7). In this case, you would want to place a limit on points to be paid.

You might want a *contingency release clause* in any contingency offer. The contingency release allows you to keep the property on the market, and gives the first offerer the right to waive his or her contingency requirement before you accept any other offer.

LOAN ASSUMPTIONS VS. WRAP-AROUND LOANS

As a buyer, you may want to take advantage of an existing below-market-rate assumable loan with a loan assumption. As a seller, the situation is different. *You* might want to retain the advantage of a below-market-rate financing when you are providing seller financing. One way to retain the advantage is by use of a *wrap-around mortgage* (also known as an "all-inclusive loan"). Under the wrap-around loan, the new loan is written for the amount of the existing loan plus the amount the seller will finance. The buyer makes payments to the seller and the seller makes the payments on the underlying loan. For example, assume a $110,000 purchase price. The buyer has a $10,000 down payment. There is an assumable $50,000 loan at 7 percent interest. A new loan could be written for $100,000 at 10 percent interest. The seller would then receive 10 percent on the $50,000 equity, plus 3 percent interest differential on the $50,000 existing loan. The seller's true interest on equity would be 13 percent.

If, in the case above, the buyer had assumed the $50,000 mortgage and had given the seller a second mortgage at 10 percent, then the buyer—not the seller—would have taken advantage of the 7 percent interest rate.

Chapter 11:
Vacation Homes

For centuries, the aristocracy of Europe have had seasonal or vacation homes. In colonial America, wealthy merchants enjoyed summer homes. They wanted to escape the congestion, smells, and heat of the summer and enjoy the recreational benefits offered by a home on the sea or in the country. A number of our resort communities were founded before the Revolutionary War.

With the upward progression of disposable income, a vacation home is one of the priority desires of Americans today. The reasons for this desire are similar to those of our colonial forefathers but vacation-home ownership also offers some very modern benefits.

TAX CONSIDERATIONS

While the Internal Revenue Service is likely to disallow business deductions for yachts and meetings on cruise ships or in exotic foreign places, there is one thoroughly pleasurable deduction that has remained largely intact. Vacation homes still offer the tax deduction of interest and property tax expenses.

If you live in your vacation home for less than 15 days a year, you can rent the property and depreciate the improvements for tax purposes. With a depreciation deduction, the vacation home will likely show a paper loss that can, subject to certain limitations, be used to offset other income; in effect, the vacation home becomes a tax shelter.

Passive Losses and Depreciation

Vacation homes did not escape the Tax Reform Act of 1986 unscathed. For instance, owners who rent out vacation homes can no longer have unlimited *passive losses*. Formerly, taxpayers could shelter other income, with some limitations, through their passive losses. Passive losses in real estate are usually noncash losses created by *depreciation*, which is a decrease in a property's value due to wear and deterioration. Depreciation is used as a paper expense to recover the cost of income and investment improvements. Under tax reform, taxpayers who have adjusted gross income less than $100,000 and who actively manage their property can offset other income up to $25,000 with passive losses. This loss is phased out between $100,000 and $150,000 in adjusted gross income. Taxpayers with greater income, as well as those who do not manage their property, may not use *any* passive losses to shelter active income. Active income includes wages, self-employment earnings, and portfolio income as well as interest. Active management means decision making. Even when an owner hires professional management, the owner still qualifies as an active manager.

If an investor who does not qualify to use a passive loss owned an investment as of the date of passage of the Tax Reform Act of 1986, the excess passive loss is phased out. In 1987, 35 percent was disallowed; in 1988, the figure rises to 60 percent; in 1989, it is 80 percent; in 1990, it is 90 percent, and in 1991 none of the passive loss in excess of income can be used.

Practically speaking, however, this change in the tax law is not really applicable to most owners of vacation homes, because most vacation homes are held for the use and enjoyment of the owners, not for rental purposes.

It is conceivable that the tax advantages currently enjoyed by vacation homeowners might be lost in the future. Analysts are predicting dire consequences should this happen. While loss of tax advantages would likely have some negative effect on the value of vacation homes, it would not be permanent.

People will still want a place to escape to. With higher disposable incomes, earlier retirements, longer life spans, and shorter work weeks, the future of vacation homes appears bright, even without the current tax advantages. In Canada, where vacation homeowners cannot deduct their interest expense, there is still a strong market for vacation homes.

APPRECIATION

In addition to interest and property tax deductions, vacation homes offer appreciation potential. Vacation homes, like other real estate, have shown a historical rate of appreciation that has exceeded inflation. Therefore, vacation homes have served many as a pleasurable hedge against inflation.

Vacation homes most likely to show the greatest amount of appreciation, like any other real estate, are those in the best locations. These homes are likely to be in greatest demand and most readily salable. As an example, a waterfront location in a water-oriented community can expect far greater appreciation than a similar home that lacks water frontage. Golf course property fronting a fairway will show far greater appreciation than homes in the same development located away from the course. Highly desirable, well-located vacation property requires a greater initial investment than less desirable vacation property that may appear to be bargain-priced; however, when it comes time to sell, the well-located, more expensive property will likely turn out to be the bargain.

ECONOMIC CHANGES

Because vacation homes are a luxury, they are more susceptible to economic changes than are homes occupied as primary residences. While values of most homes might remain stable or show a slight decline during a recessionary period, the value of vacation homes is likely to undergo a much sharper decline. The reason for this is that during a recessionary period, a great many people tighten their belts and eliminate luxuries. Vacation homes purchased during good times are placed on the market by owners who are forced to sell. The market forces of supply and demand result in the lowering of prices. For a buyer, the best time to buy a vacation home would be during a recession. For a seller, the best time to sell a vacation home would be during a period of general prosperity.

FINANCING

Because vacation-home values react more directly to economic changes, loan qualifications for these types of homes tend to be tougher. A lender who might be willing to finance 85 percent of the price of a primary residence might offer to finance only 75 percent of the cost of the same home when purchased as a second home. Interest rates on second homes are often one-half to one percent higher than for primary residences. This increased interest is charged by lenders who consider a vacation-home loan a greater risk.

Owner Financing

Because of tighter lender financing, owner financing is more prevalent on vacation home sales than for primary residences. Sellers of vacation homes are less likely to need the cash than are sellers of primary residences. Often they are selling simply to reduce their expenses. Such sellers are not only more willing to finance buyers, they will usually do so at an attractive rate of interest.

TIME-SHARES

Time-shares are interval ownership projects whereby a time-share owner gets exclusive possession of the property during an agreed time period each year. Typically, time-shares are resort-type properties. Time-share interest might be fee ownership that continues indefinitely, transferable by deed or inheritance, or it could be a leasehold interest for a certain period, such as 50 years. At the end of the leasehold, all interest in the property customarily reverts to the original owner.

Don't regard a time-share as an investment. While a few very desirable developments have experienced an increase in value, most time-share resales have been for considerably less than the original sale price. For many people, however, time-shares make sense. For a set fee, owners can lock in their future vacations to their share of the operational costs. For a person with only two weeks of vacation each year, a time-share may make more sense than total ownership of a vacation home.